TEACHING ADVANCED LITERACY SKILLS

Also from Nonie K. Lesaux and Sky H. Marietta

Making Assessment Matter:
Using Test Results to Differentiate Reading Instruction

Teaching Advanced Literacy Skills

A Guide for Leaders in Linguistically Diverse Schools

Nonie K. Lesaux
Emily Phillips Galloway
Sky H. Marietta

THE GUILFORD PRESS
New York   London

© 2016 The Guilford Press
A Division of Guilford Publications, Inc.
370 Seventh Avenue, Suite 1200, New York, NY 10001
www.guilford.com

Printed in the United States of America

This book is printed on acid-free paper.

Last digit is print number: 9   8   7   6   5   4   3   2   1

Library of Congress Cataloging-in-Publication Data

Names: Lesaux, Nonie K., author. | Galloway, Emily Phillips, author. |
    Marietta, Sky H., author.
Title: Teaching advanced literacy skills : a guide for leaders in
    linguistically diverse schools / Nonie K. Lesaux, Emily Phillips Galloway,
    Sky H. Marietta.
Description: New York : Guilford Press, [2016] | Includes bibliographical
    references and index.
Identifiers: LCCN 2016022050| ISBN 9781462526468 (pbk. : alk. paper) | ISBN
    9781462526475 (hardcover : alk. paper)
Subjects: LCSH: Language arts—United States. | Linguistic
    minorities—Education—United States. | Common Core State Standards
    (Education) | School management and organization.
Classification: LCC LB1576 .L4844 2016 | DDC 372.6—dc23
LC record available at *https://lccn.loc.gov/2016022050*

About the Authors

Nonie K. Lesaux, PhD, is the Juliana W. and William Foss Thompson Professor of Education and Society at the Harvard Graduate School of Education. Dr. Lesaux leads a research program guided by the goal of increasing opportunities to learn for students from diverse linguistic, cultural, and economic backgrounds. Her work on reading development and instruction, and on using data to prevent reading difficulties, informs setting-level interventions and public policy at the national and state levels. The practical applications of this work are featured in numerous publications, including the books *Making Assessment Matter* and *Cultivating Knowledge, Building Language*, as well as a widely circulated state literacy report, *Turning the Page: Refocusing Massachusetts for Reading Success*, that forms the basis for a third-grade reading proficiency bill passed in Massachusetts. Dr. Lesaux is a recipient of the William T. Grant Scholars award from the William T. Grant Foundation and of the Presidential Early Career Award for Scientists and Engineers, the highest honor given by the United States government to young professionals beginning their independent research careers.

Emily Phillips Galloway, EdD, is Assistant Professor at Vanderbilt University's Peabody College of Education and Human Development. Inspired by her work as a former middle school reading specialist and English language arts teacher, Dr. Galloway conducts research on the development of the language skills that support advanced literacy in struggling readers and in linguistically diverse adolescents. In addition, she works with large urban districts, school leaders, and educators to design literacy improvement efforts and assessment systems.

Sky H. Marietta, EdD, is the Curriculum and Instruction Specialist at Pine Mountain Settlement School, a not-for-profit organization focused on improving opportunities for children in Appalachia, and a research fellow at Berea College. Previously, she was a postdoctoral fellow and lecturer at the Harvard Graduate School of Education. Dr. Marietta's work examines connections among language, culture, poverty, and reading achievement, with a special emphasis on rural populations and science literacy. A former elementary teacher, she has worked with numerous teachers and districts on implementing efficient and informative literacy assessment systems. She is coauthor with Nonie K. Lesaux of *Making Assessment Matter*.

Acknowledgments

With immigration and migration a part of the societal fabric and the seismic shifts in how information is gathered and transmitted, it's a new world for education. In classrooms around the globe, the learners sitting in chairs and working at tables are increasingly diverse. For many of these children, the classroom marks their first encounter with the language of schooling, which complicates the learning task for students and teachers. At the same time, in these same classrooms, the substance of daily instruction is also changing. The role that information and communication play in daily life has been transformed in ways that were never predicted a century ago, and our educational model is racing to catch up.

Our inspiration for this book grew out of a multiyear partnership—one in which we worked to support literacy leaders and create schools and classrooms that reflect what we know from our own and others' research on literacy learning for linguistically diverse students. From this partnership, which involved nearly 50 school leaders and district administrators in one of the largest, most linguistically diverse urban districts in the United States, we came to understand the challenges and see the possibilities for ensuring that literacy instruction satisfies what it means to be "literate" today, while also supporting the growing number of linguistically diverse students in our schools. Through this partnership, which most often took the form of in-depth team-based work guided by the latest evidence, we designed the model for advanced literacy instructional leadership that we present here.

As this book goes to press, we wish to thank many individuals for their collaboration and partnership in the collective effort. Angelica Infante championed this initiative in the earliest years; in the district, she impressed a strong view that the principles of adult learning and the data on English language learners must be at the core of all professional learning. We also thank the many principals, instructional leaders, and teachers with whom we've had the opportunity to collaborate. For many, improving teaching and learning for their students guides not just their work, but also their mind-sets. At the Harvard Graduate School of Education, we have the privilege of learning from a tremendous group of colleagues in the Language Diversity and Literacy Development research group. We thank each of them for ongoing discussion and collaboration that fuels our thinking and work. We also thank Craig Thomas of The Guilford Press for his investment in our work. Finally, it is Stela Radovanovic to whom we are most indebted. Stela has been a partner in implementation for several years. It is a pleasure and a privilege to work with someone as talented and thoughtful as Stela, and her insights about literacy reform and support for students needing to acquire the academic language of schooling has informed our understanding of today's literacy landscape. In closing, we dedicate this book to the school leaders who have inspired us along the way.

Contents

PART II. Leading the Implementation
of Four Key Site-Based Shifts for Progress

PART III. Moving Forward at a School Site

Purchasers of this book can download and print the Leader's Tools
at *www.guilford.com/lesaux2-forms*
for personal use or use with individual students.

PART I

Advanced Literacies for the 21st Century

CHAPTER 1

Rethinking Literacy and Its Leadership
for the 21st Century

Today's school leaders—especially those serving large numbers of linguistically diverse learners—face a "new" normal that guides their instructional work. To be academically and personally successful in today's literacy- and knowledge-based society and economy, each of their students need to develop what we refer to as *advanced literacies*. This term denotes skills and competencies that enable communication, spoken and written, in increasingly diverse ways and with increasingly diverse audiences. Advanced literacies also promote the understanding and use of text for a variety of purposes. Likewise they make way for participation in academic, civic, and professional communities, where knowledge is shared and generated (Organization for Economic Cooperation and Development [OECD], 2010).

Reading and writing—language-based competencies—have become prerequisites for participation in nearly every aspect of day-to-day, 21st-century life. There was a time when basic literacy skills provided a clear path forward, when extended reading and writing were the business of education and only necessary for participation in white-collar professions. But today, students need to develop an increasingly complex set of advanced literacy skills and competencies in order to access social and economic opportunities. Importantly, the press for advanced literacies for all does not reflect a decline in the population's literacy rates. Instead it is recognition that what counts as "literate" has changed dramatically over the last few decades (Levy & Murnane, 2005).

The urgent call for instruction to promote advanced literacies among all students comes at a time when the system is already charged with building

3

up language skills among the increasingly linguistically diverse population. English learners (ELs) now comprise over 20% of the school-age population, which reflects significant growth in the past several decades. Between 1980 and 2009, this population increased from 4.7 to 11.2 million young people, or from 10 to 21% of the school-age population. The greatest growth has occurred in our secondary schools (Garcia & Cuéllar, 2006). This growth will likely continue in U.S. schools; by 2030, it is anticipated that 40% of the school-age population in the United States will speak a language other than English at home (Camarota, 2012). Today, in schools and districts across the United States, many students other than those formally classified as ELs are learning English as an additional language, even if not in the initial stages of language development—these children are often described as "language-minority learners." Likewise we increasingly find students who speak a nonmainstream dialect of English that is different from the academic English found in school curricula (Washington, Terry, & Seidenberg, 2013).[1]

Across these three groups large numbers are growing up in poverty (Aud et al., 2011); and we know that because of what James Ryan has dubbed the "politics of separation" in the United States (2010, p. 13), these learners tend to cluster in neighborhoods and therefore in schools. This has important implications for literacy instruction. In our own work, we find that in high-poverty settings, each of these groups—ELs, language minority learners, and nonmainstream dialect speakers—*and* their native English-speaking peers often

WHAT DO WE MEAN BY "ADVANCED LITERACIES"?

Advanced literacy is a term we will use often in this book, and that we describe in more detail in the next chapter. When we say "advanced literacy," we mean much more than decoding and understanding print; we are focused on the new role that language and literacy skills take in society—in our neighborhoods and in the global world—and what this means for classroom instruction. Today's students need to develop increasingly sophisticated literacy skills to thrive day-to-day; they need to communicate (orally and in writing) in increasingly diverse ways and with increasingly diverse audiences; they also need to understand and use print for a variety of purposes. To be successful in school and beyond, from the earliest of years, our students need to develop the skills and knowledge that go into advanced literacy.

---

[1]Nonmainstream dialects of English include African American English (AAE), Southern White English (SWE), and Southern African American English (SAAE) (Wolfram & Schilling-Estes, 1998).

struggle to access the language, and therefore the knowledge, that fills the pages of academic texts (Kieffer & Vukovic, 2012; Lesaux & Kieffer, 2010).

The goal of promoting advanced literacies among all students—including those that are linguistically diverse—reflected in legislation, policies, and initiatives reveals a growing awareness that it is both possible and necessary to make schooling more equitable, which begins by having high expectations for our students' literacy attainment. Problematically, little concrete guidance has been provided to support progress toward this goal on the ground. This leaves many dedicated, hard-working school leaders and educators with the question: *What is the best strategy for getting there?*

There is no single answer to this question given the complexity of the task. In this book we begin the work of guiding school leaders to create the conditions at their school sites that promote advanced literacies instruction— teaching that fits a new reality of increasing linguistic diversity. In taking this issue on and providing practical guidance, we are not motivated by the standards of today. Rather we look ahead, mindful that society will increasingly prioritize and value the development of advanced literacies for *all* students.

What Does "Advanced Literacies for All" Mean for School Leaders?

Meeting today's demands for what counts as "literate" requires a new approach to instructional leadership for school leaders; they must drastically change the way their schools organize for and approach instruction. For example, the needs of linguistically diverse students have typically been addressed through instructional approaches that take place on the margins, rather than at the core of daily instruction activity. In many schools, a small cadre of specialists in second-language or literacy development have been largely responsible for the language and literacy development of ELs and struggling readers— and they have provided this instruction outside of the content-area classroom (Heritage, Walqui, & Linquanti, 2015). This is evidence that language and content teaching are typically viewed as separate and, on that basis, intervention for struggling readers is not integrated with the instructional core (Lesaux & Marietta, 2011).

Instead, teaching for advanced literacies demands what van Lier and Walqui (2012) characterize as a movement away from the conventional practice of teaching "language in isolation" from content learning. It's now recognized that, if we are to equip students with the linguistic tools needed to express their content knowledge, then reading, writing, and speaking must be taught in the content-rich elementary classroom or in the secondary disciplinary classroom (Lemke, 1990; Hull & Moje, 2012). And for those who are struggling with acquiring language and with their foundational skills, there is a significant need to integrate the intervention with daily instruction.

Schools have generally not been organized to support this highly collaborative instruction, nor have most teachers and administrators had sufficient opportunity to cultivate the understanding of literacy and language development needed to craft it. As a result, U.S. schools struggle to provide opportunities for linguistically diverse students to develop the literacy skills and competencies necessary to learn from text and to express their knowledge orally and in writing.

Meeting today's demands for what counts as "literate" therefore requires a bold new approach to instructional leadership, especially for school leaders who are serving large numbers of linguistically diverse learners. In this book,

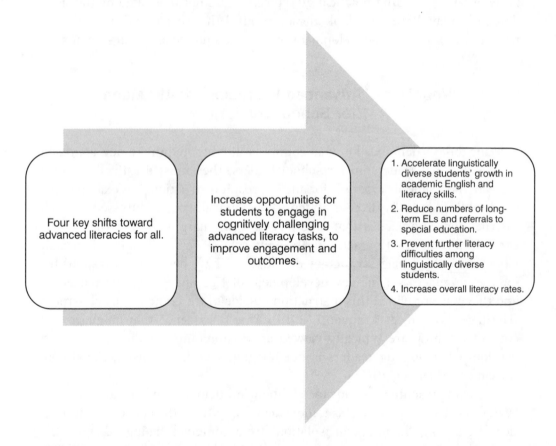

FIGURE 1.1. A theory of action for instructional leaders in linguistically diverse settings.

we identify and explain four shifts that support this instructional leadership. Following our theory of action (see Figure 1.1), these shifts lead to increased opportunities for linguistically diverse learners to develop advanced literacies. The larger result would be improved literacy performance among these populations.

Working at the Nexus of Existing Initiatives and Goals to Achieve Advanced Literacies for All

The challenge of reorganizing to promote advanced literacies for all is compounded by the rapid pace with which initiatives enter and exit our schools, forcing educators and leaders to continually play catch-up. It has been our experience that educators and school leaders already work very hard without getting the intended and desired outcome of advanced literacies for all. *Simply working longer or harder is not the answer; working more strategically is indeed a key answer.* This is difficult, however, given the way in which policies and initiatives are presented as independent in nature and unrelated to one another. We have a standards-based reform movement in the United States, symbolized by the Common Core State Standards, which aim to prepare students for college and career opportunities. Other large-scale reforms include the No Child Left Behind Act (2001) and the more recent response-to-intervention (RTI) model. Together, these reforms share the goal of promoting advanced literacies for *all* students, regardless of disability/language status, family income, or race and ethnicity. Yet conceptualizing these initiatives without a single architecture to guide their implementation has in many settings—especially those considered "underperforming"—caused undue expenditure of time, resources, and energy, ultimately impeding the collective goal of these efforts.

Working more strategically begins with recognizing what these initiatives all share as a desired end result—improving literacy rates among all students—and working tirelessly toward achieving this goal, even as new initiatives enter the educational landscape. For this reason, our focus throughout this book is on strong instructional design, and, as a *consequence*, meeting standards and mandated initiatives. Drawing on our experience working with schools, we suggest putting instruction into place that will meet three pressing goals: (1) to promote advanced literacies for all students; (2) to better link data and instruction for the purposes of achievement and evaluation; and (3) to meet the demands of standards-based reform—both today's standards and those that will inevitably follow in their wake. As shown in Figure 1.2, at the nexus of these three goals is the powerful brand of advanced literacies instruction we describe in this book.

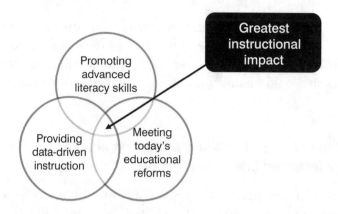

FIGURE 1.2. Powerful instruction for advanced literacies.

Working more strategically to lead instruction for advanced literacies also opens up an opportunity to capitalize on the strengths and learning profiles of these students. Language-minority learners, for instance, demonstrate relative strengths in the face of what appears to be lower academic attainment overall, on average. In other words, there are benefits to navigating two or more languages or dialects. For instance, among language-minority learners (ELs and their peers who have never been classified as such), by the end of second grade with adequate instructional opportunities, most show the basic ability to decode (or read) printed words (e.g., Geva & Yaghoub Zadeh, 2006; Lesaux, Lipka, & Siegel, 2006; Mancilla-Martinez & Lesaux, 2011). Thus, despite having to simultaneously acquire the language of schooling *and* early literacy skills, these learners master these skills within the same time frame as their peers from middle-class, majority-culture backgrounds (August & Shanahan, 2006; Lesaux, Rupp, & Siegel, 2007). In fact, many even demonstrate heightened ability on measures of their knowledge of how language works and on their cognitive flexibility (e.g., Bialystok, Craik, & Luk, 2012; Lesaux & Siegel, 2003). True, the competencies that are even more directly related to text comprehension, such as vocabulary and academic language knowledge, are persistent sources of difficulty for these students, especially after elementary school (Lesaux, Kieffer, Faller, & Kelley, 2010). But what's important to note is that ELs' *rates* of growth in these areas most often surpasses the national rate of growth (Kieffer, 2008). This is great news on its face, but the problem is that this growth is still not fast enough to get these students to grade level. The challenge and corresponding opportunity we thus face in our schools is *to shift our instructional model to capitalize on these relative strengths, while bolstering areas of academic vulnerability.*

A Map of This Book

In the chapters that follow, we provide guidance to school leaders charged with crafting a site-level approach—the architecture or blueprint—for developing advanced literacies among all students, especially those developing their academic English. We have written this book as a guide that ensures that the resulting approach is one that attends to the needs of all learners in the school building—students *and* adults.

As shown in Figure 1.3, the book is divided into three parts. Part I (Chapters 1–3) focuses on advanced literacies for the 21st century. Across these three

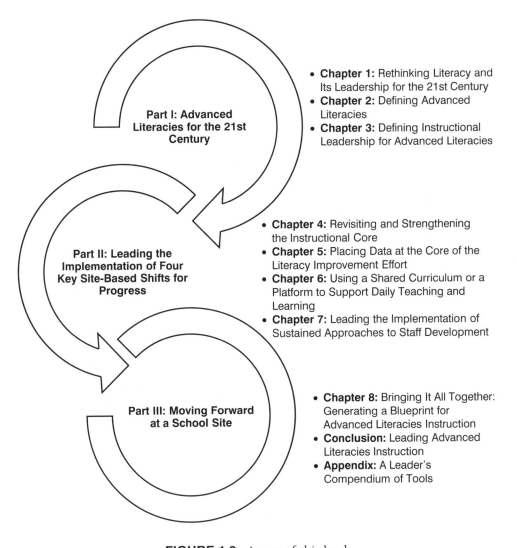

Part I: Advanced Literacies for the 21st Century

- **Chapter 1:** Rethinking Literacy and Its Leadership for the 21st Century
- **Chapter 2:** Defining Advanced Literacies
- **Chapter 3:** Defining Instructional Leadership for Advanced Literacies

Part II: Leading the Implementation of Four Key Site-Based Shifts for Progress

- **Chapter 4:** Revisiting and Strengthening the Instructional Core
- **Chapter 5:** Placing Data at the Core of the Literacy Improvement Effort
- **Chapter 6:** Using a Shared Curriculum or a Platform to Support Daily Teaching and Learning
- **Chapter 7:** Leading the Implementation of Sustained Approaches to Staff Development

Part III: Moving Forward at a School Site

- **Chapter 8:** Bringing It All Together: Generating a Blueprint for Advanced Literacies Instruction
- **Conclusion:** Leading Advanced Literacies Instruction
- **Appendix:** A Leader's Compendium of Tools

FIGURE 1.3. A map of this book.

chapters, we discuss 21st-century literacy demands and what we mean by "advanced literacies," whether we're talking about the implementation of this instruction in the upper elementary or the middle school setting. To offer concrete guidance in creating the site-level conditions that promote advanced literacies, we profile four key shifts that school leaders should undertake related to (1) curricular plans and materials in use at the school site; (2) day-to-day instruction and pedagogy; (3) student assessment data-to-instruction links; (4) and professional learning for faculty and staff. Part II (Chapters 4–7) offers concrete guidance for implementing these key shifts as part of a strong leadership approach for promoting advanced literacies day to day and across the year, with a deep focus on the instructional core and sustained staff development, and an emphasis on data-driven decisions that will inform the design of instruction that matches students' needs. In this section, we include tools for self-study to support the leader in assessing the current status of instruction that supports advanced literacies at his or her site and lead the implementation of needed shifts. Part III (Chapter 8 and Conclusion), the final section of the book, focuses on helping leaders get started with a major literacy reform effort at their school site; after all, it's only with a site-based approach that the goal of advanced literacies for all will be accomplished. Chapter 8 begins by revisiting the main issues to be addressed if we are to get to advanced literacies for all. Next, the chapter supports the leader in generating a blueprint that outlines specific action steps and decision making about priorities and instructional approaches for site-based improvement. We follow with the case example of the Rosa Parks School—a K–8 school with a typical middle school structure for grades 6–8. In highlighting key elements of the advanced literacies reform process at Rosa Parks, we draw distinctions between their work in the upper elementary schools (grades 3–5), where one teachers serves the students in a classroom, and their work in the middle school (grades 6–8), where students rotate through classrooms (and teachers) by content area. The Conclusion ends this section with a very brief summary of the issues and key strategies outlined in the preceding chapters. Finally, the Appendix features a compendium of tools for the leader, making accessible in one place all resources from this book, to support site-level efforts.

Our Case School

To center our work in the school-based context, we use the case example of the Rosa Parks School. A composite of many schools, administrators, teachers, and students with whom we have worked over the years, Rosa Parks is a K–8 school in a large, urban district. Rosa Parks serves mostly linguistically diverse students (nearly 75% are ELs). Mirroring the demographics of the United States, the vast majority of EL students and bilingual teachers at the school speak Spanish as their first language (Aud et al., 2011), but many of these same students are said to be mostly English-only by the time they reach middle school, on account of the language of instruction (English) and the neighborhood (also English). Other students (and teachers) are speakers of nonmainstream dialects of English in their homes and communities.

Under the leadership of Principal Mary Lansdowne, Rosa Parks has worked to create an environment that is supportive of language learning, which has meant embracing research-based understandings. Because an important principle at Rosa Parks is that development of a first language supports development in a second (an idea now well established in research; see, e.g., Genesee, Geva, Dressler, & Kamil, 2006), parents are encouraged to work with children around literacy activities using the language in which they are most fluent. In addition, given their strengths-based orientation, teachers frequently refer to students' errors when speaking English in the classroom as "clues" about their language development, which they use to inform instruction (de Jong & Harper, 2004). Students are also provided with formal support for English language development via pullout instruction provided by specialists and through participation in after-school, computer-based tutoring.

Despite these efforts, students' performance on state assessments have remained stagnant: nearly 80% have performed below grade level for the last 5 years. Serving 800 children across 30 classrooms, Rosa Parks is struggling to meet the needs of its students, most of whom are growing up in poverty (over 95% of students at the school this year are eligible for free or reduced-price lunches); in the district, resources—time, personnel, and finances—are scarce and expectations for student success only growing. Like many of our partner schools, Rosa Parks has been inundated with initiatives, most of which come with little support for implementation; the faculty, comprised of over 40 teachers, reading specialists, and English language specialists, though deeply committed to students, have grown weary of the steady parade of new programs, curricula, and interventions.

The Inspiration for This Book:
A Partnership with a Large Urban District

Before we move on, we would like to explain our inspiration for this book, which grew out of a multiyear partnership with nearly 50 school leaders and district administrators in one of the largest, most linguistically diverse urban districts in the United States. It was through this partnership, which most often took the form of in-depth team-based work over several days at a time, that we designed the model for advanced literacy instructional leadership that we present here.

Too often in education, knowledge lives in silos and research doesn't find its way into practice. In many instances, our work has highlighted school leaders' difficulties in determining which new practices and programs are evidence-based amid the press to rapidly adopt new practices that might benefit teachers and learners. Here, we commit to and focus on a systemic, sustained approach to supporting advanced literacy development in upper elementary through middle school that does not privilege any one ideology or movement; instead, it draws on the science of reading and its instruction, on the science of language acquisition (whether first or second) and dialectical differences, and on attending to the real-world context of instructional practice and especially urban education reform, by incorporating the key lessons from our colleagues who are experts in this area.

To this district partnership, we brought a range of professional experiences. We all started our careers working with children and continue to do so. Nonie was an educational psychologist in an urban school district focused on preventing early reading difficulties, and still provides consultations on specific cases of struggling readers. She leads a program of research focused on the literacy development and difficulties faced by ELs and their monolingual peers, and designs effective instructional environments to increase opportunities to learn for these populations. Emily was a literacy specialist and middle school teacher. Her research focuses on sharpening our understanding of the role of academic language in reading comprehension, including how academic language should be measured and taught. Sky was an elementary teacher who still collaborates regularly with teachers and schools. She investigates the home language and print experiences of young children, how these home experiences intersect with instruction, and how teachers can bridge cultural divides. We worked together as members of the Language and Literacy Program at the Harvard Graduate School of Education, where we taught classes that train future teachers, literacy specialists, and educational researchers. Among us, we have worked in urban, rural, and suburban contexts, most often with leaders and teachers whose students face many challenges in learning to read complex academic texts. And, yet, it was work with our partners in this urban district that forced us to think most creatively and strategically about the problems of leadership and practice that we tackle in this book. We thank them for this challenge and opportunity.

Of course, our experience served to highlight the reality that there are no easy solutions to the problems and challenges one faces when preparing students for complex, academic ways of speaking, reading, and writing. However, we are excited to provide leaders with knowledge and tools that will promote advanced literacies within a district, school, or classroom. It is our belief that the architecture we provide in this book is a powerful one—one that supports educational practitioners and leaders by equipping them with the knowledge to feel confident and capable of leading the design of learning environments where students are acquiring the literacy-based skills and competencies demanded by today's global society.

CHAPTER 2

Defining Advanced Literacies

In the fourth- through eighth-grade classrooms at Rosa Parks School, all students were preparing for a debate centered on the question: Should we have to wear a school uniform? This was a hot topic given that the principal had declared the policy open to review. The students had read newspaper articles on the topic and written letters to the editor. The assigned articles and essays had proven influential. In some cases, after encountering arguments and ideas about how clothing can serve to unite and divide groups, students had gained new perspectives and switched sides in the controversy.

In preparation for the debate, using supports such as graphic organizers, the students had prepared their arguments—writing down their main points, rationale, and evidence. After the debates concluded, each student was to write an essay on the topic, but as a prewriting exercise students engaged in a discussion about communicating with their audience. Some were writing to persuade a group of peers and others were writing directly to the principal and the school board. Given these different audiences, teachers focused on supporting students to use the language needed to engage and persuade their particular readers.

As we move beyond equipping students with foundational literacy skills to models of instruction like the one described above, we must be clear what is meant by "advanced literacies." These skills and competencies support each of us to communicate (orally and in writing) in increasingly diverse ways and with increasingly diverse audiences; to understand and use print for a variety of purposes; and to access and participate in academic, civic, and professional communities, where knowledge is shared and generated. As shown in Figure 2.1, without question advanced literacies play a larger role in one's academic and personal success in today's knowledge-based society and economy than in decades past, but this does not mean that we in the field of education have adequately answered questions central to their instruction in classroom settings—for instance, "What, exactly, are the specific skills and competencies that support advanced literacies?" and "What does this instruction look like?" Indeed, there are many skills and competencies that go into what we call advanced literacies that must be cultivated in the classroom and must continue to develop throughout life. At their core is the need for a strong command of language—both oral and written. This need adds to the complexity of literacy reform in any setting with large numbers of linguistically diverse learners.

Organization of This Chapter

In this chapter, with supporting examples, we describe in detail key skills and competencies that we aim to foster among all students so that they can participate in advanced literacies tasks. In so doing, we draw a critical distinction between what we call "component skills" and "composite competencies." As part of this discussion, we focus on "academic language skills," which despite being a buzzword in our field today has not necessarily been clearly defined for operation in classroom practice. The information in this chapter is intended to help leaders select literacy reform initiatives to implement. The

Advanced Literacies in Academic Contexts

- Writing an argumentative essay or lab report that draws on text-based or empirical evidence.
- Participating in a class discussion or debate.
- Synthesizing information across a series of texts.
- Listening to and understanding a class lecture or discussion.

Advanced Literacies in Civic and Professional Contexts

- Writing an op-ed piece or article.
- Making an oral presentation.
- Reading pamphlets and literature about personal or child health and applying this knowledge.
- Listening to and understanding news media.

FIGURE 2.1. Advanced literacies in academic and civic/professional contexts.

more desirable initiatives will be rooted in research and will likely contribute to growth in students' advanced literacies. As a preview of the remaining chapters in Part I and all chapters in Part II, we close this chapter with some of the traditional instructional practices that are common in schools today but which fall short of our 21st-century goals for instruction, focusing on key composite competencies.

Advanced Literacies: Component Skills and Composite Competencies

In designing a plan that provides comprehensive instruction to promote advanced literacies for all, understanding the distinction between component skills and composite competencies is crucial. As shown in Figure 2.2, *component skills* refer to very specific literacy skills (e.g., learning to match

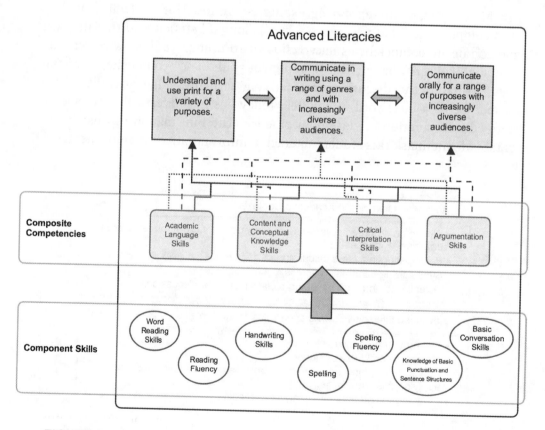

FIGURE 2.2. Advanced literacies: Component skills and composite competencies.

sounds to letters so as to read or spell words, or learning how to make sense of basic punctuation in a text). We can think of these skills as related to the "mechanical" aspects of reading, writing, and speaking in that they are necessary for us to read words, write words, and hear individual words in a stream of speech. They are associated with basic literacy skills, but they also support one's execution of real-world literacy tasks. *Composite competencies* are the sum or "composite" of many foundational skills working in combination with the higher-order skills. They are central to advanced literacies, whether to comprehend and synthesize sophisticated text, construct knowledge when writing, or engage in an academic debate. As our component skills develop, we are in a better position to develop composite competencies, but the latter also demand even more intensive and varied experiences interacting with text, language, and the broader world. For example, content and conceptual knowledge, which supports us in understanding what we read, begins to develop as soon as we are exposed to language as infants. It continues to evolve in the conversations we have as young children, and advances further as we engage in print-based discussions about content in the classroom.

To delve into this notion of advanced literacies and the component skills and composite competencies of which they are comprised, let's start with an example of the difference between foundational, or basic, literacy skills and advanced literacies. To demonstrate the former, we might ask a fourth grader to read and summarize in a few sentences the "main idea" of a passage, drawn from a straightforward text on a familiar topic. Taking an advanced literacies frame, we might ask this student to use the information in that same straightforward text in combination with information found in two more complex texts to make a reasoned argument when writing an essay. For the latter, he or she will have to use all the skills that supported him or her in literally comprehending the first text; but to be successful in accomplishing this task, he or she will also draw on some *key composite competencies* of advanced literacies— academic language skills, content and conceptual knowledge, critical interpretation, and argumentation skill. He or she will need to engage in learning from, analyzing, and critiquing text as well as conveying these understandings in writing.

In schools serving large numbers of linguistically diverse students, whether ELs or students who are acquiring academic English as a second dialect, data often suggest that the majority need significantly more support to develop the composite competencies that play a crucial role in one's advanced literacies (Compton, Miller, Elleman, & Steacy, 2014; Kieffer & Vokovic, 2012; Uccelli, Galloway, Barr, Meneses, & Dobbs, 2015). By the upper elementary and middle school years, while a group of students will invariably need more intense support for developing component skills, this group is typically a whole lot smaller than the group needing support for composite competencies. It is the composite competencies that are both a gateway and a gatekeeper for many students vis-à-vis academic success, and this is especially the case for our linguistically diverse population. On average, ELs and their peers who speak a nonmainstream dialect of English have fewer opportunities to be exposed to and to use academic language, which is so often found in texts at school.

However, we are clear that these generally lower rates in the composite competencies do not signal a learning problem among these students. We see evidence of this in a 10-year longitudinal study following Spanish-speaking children from age 4 (all United States-born children of immigrants recruited from Head Start early learning centers) through early adolescence conducted by Mancilla-Martinez and Lesaux (2010). The study found that, when entering middle school, these students' component skills were well within the average ranges while their composite competencies, such as vocabulary knowledge, were well below average, around the 20th percentile. But it wasn't a problem with *rate* of growth, or learning, per se. That is, these students advanced at a rate equivalent to that of the average U.S. monolingual English student. So why the low levels of achievement? It's a question of the starting point: the rate of growth these students exhibited wasn't fast *enough* to get them where they needed to be, given that they began school with lower proficiency in English than their English-only peers. They were acquiring English language skills quickly—but not quickly enough to close this early gap, which persists over time; bear in mind that their English-only learners continue to acquire language too. If our linguistically diverse students are going to get to advanced literacies, their rate of growth in acquiring the skills and knowledge needed to read and produce complex text will need to be even faster—and here we turn to our instructional model and the need to bring it up to date to match today's students and today's literacy demands. Before moving on to what this means for instruction—a different model altogether, indeed—let's delve into those key competencies that are proving particularly challenging for ELs and their peers as they seek to acquire the language of schooling.

Four Key Composite Competencies Unpacked

Given the challenges associated with developing advanced literacies, we focus here on four key composite competencies that support this development: (1) *academic language skills*; (2) *content and conceptual knowledge*; (3) *critical interpretation skills*; and (4) *argumentation skills*. This is not intended to be an exhaustive list, but rather a focus on those competencies that are crucial if we are to begin to raise literacy rates in settings serving large numbers of linguistically diverse students. Below we discuss each composite competency in turn, highlighting what we know about its development and its relationship to advanced literacies. But here is one final note before we dig in: while we present these as competencies that can be readily distinguished for the purposes of this discussion and for designing assessment and instruction, in reality, of course, most advanced literacies tasks call on all these competencies simultaneously.

Academic Language Skills

Welcome. The background for today's debate is a policy decision in our school that will affect the students. The principal is deciding about whether the students will have to wear a uniform every day, beginning next year. Today we will hear from individuals representing both sides of the argument. Each presenter will have 5 minutes to make his or her case and then we will have a question-and-answer session. Let's proceed.
—PHUONG, seventh-grade EL and debate moderator

As an EL, preparing for and moderating this debate is stretching Phuong's academic language competencies. She drafted and revised, then practiced and practiced to fulfill the demands of the role. Most of her revisions focused on what the class had been working on—using academic words and phrases instead of everyday language. In doing that work, Phuong had replaced "on both" with "representing both," replaced "person" with "presenter," replaced "start" with "proceed," and replaced "matter for" with "affect."

For young children and adolescents alike, academic success means having command of academic language—an essential tool for reading, writing, and critical thinking. This is the language used and valued for communicative purposes in secondary school, higher education, and many professional settings; it is the language of school texts and assessments and of the scholarly world (Nagy & Townsend, 2012; Scarcella, 2003). It is also the language used in the media and society at large for communicating complex information—such as health-related data and political ideas. To read and write across content areas, a student needs well-developed academic language skills. In this sense, we can think of academic language as a *gatekeeper* and as a *gateway*. When academic language is largely inaccessible, so too is the school curriculum; accessing the language, though, means having the chance to learn academic concepts and to generate ideas and questions that contribute to academic conversations. Ultimately it means having a chance to achieve academically.

How does *academic* language relate to language skills generally? Well, when we use language, knitting together words and phrases to communicate our thoughts, the elements can take on fewer or more of the characteristics that are typical of academic text and talk. In that sense, the way we think of it is that language is the musical range of a singing voice and academic language is one "register." By register, we mean language used for a specific purpose or in a specific social setting—and characterized by a particular set of characteristics and traits (Schleppegrell, 2004). In our daily lives, whether speaking or writing, we may switch registers, moving from an academic one to a more informal casual one and vice versa, throughout the day. The characteristics of academic language are often described as existing on one end of a continuum, with everyday, social, conversational language at the other extreme (Snow, 2010).

We've often been asked to enumerate the words, phrases, and sentence structures that can be called "academic language." However, because language exists on a continuum from less academic to more academic, it is impractical (even impossible) to generate a laundry list of *all* academic language features (Snow & Uccelli, 2009). But a number of characteristics, together, make academic language *academic*. Bear in mind, for example, that in everyday spoken language, we make use of shorter sentences and familiar words. We can clarify our meaning, offer additional information, or repeat a statement if the listener becomes confused—none of these steps are possible when we are writing or delivering a formal speech, which is one reason that academic writing favors the use of precise, explicit, and concise language.

Keeping in mind that some aspects of academic language vary among the content areas (even among text genres), we focus on those characteristics of academic language that are considered common across the curriculum. In particular, we highlight four components of academic language (syntax, morphology, pragmatics, and vocabulary knowledge) that support our students in order to communicate and learn content delivered orally and to understand the language of print.

The first three—syntax, morphology, and pragmatics skills—are central for putting together and taking apart the meaning of sentences and longer texts, both oral and written. *Syntax* refers to a student's understanding of grammatical rules and word order (Moats, 2000). In some cases, changing the order of the words does not change the meaning—in other cases, a small change can alter what a sentence is communicating (e.g., The boy hit the ball; The ball hit the boy). Syntax knowledge begins to develop as students are exposed to spoken language; this development continues as they become readers and encounter sentence structures that are rare in spoken language.

Morphology skill refers to a reader's knowledge of the smallest meaningful parts of a word, including roots, suffixes, and prefixes (Moats, 2010). When a reader encounters a word that is unfamiliar to him or her (e.g., *unpredictable*) in spoken or written language, he or she can make use of his or her morphology knowledge to infer the word's meaning. For instance, he or she might understand how a particular prefix or suffix (e.g., *un-* and *-able*) changes the meaning of a word or he or she might know that two words with the same root may have similar meanings (e.g., *predict, predictable, unpredictable*). For ELs and monolingual English speakers, strong morphological awareness correlates with reading comprehension (Carlisle, 2000; Deacon & Kirby, 2004; Goodwin, Huggins, Carlo, August, & Calderon, 2013; Kieffer, Biancarosa, & Mancilla-Martinez, 2013; Nagy, Berninger, & Abbott, 2006; Pacheco & Goodwin, 2013).

Pragmatics refers to our understanding of the social rules of communication. Pragmatics involves how we adjust our language when we have a particular purpose (e.g., convincing someone vs. comforting them); the niceties we might use to communicate when we're speaking with a particular audience (e.g., a friend vs. an employer); and what we say when we find ourselves in certain social contexts (e.g., an informal conversation over coffee vs. a formal presentation at work). It seems that pragmatics would have little to do with text comprehension, except that extracting meaning from text—understanding the feelings or reactions of a character or group—depends upon how familiar the reader is with the norms for interacting with others through language that are implicit within texts (Britton & Graesser, 2014; Vipond & Hunt, 1984). In addition, our pragmatic knowledge supports our students in adjusting their language when writing and speaking for different audiences.

The fourth and perhaps most fundamental component of academic language (as well as of reading and writing) is *vocabulary knowledge*, which involves both understanding what words and phrases mean (receptive vocabulary) *and* using those words and phrases to effectively communicate with others (expressive vocabulary). Though we rarely think of it this way, vocabulary knowledge exists in degrees, such that an individual for any given word has a particular "level" of knowledge (Beck, McKeown, & Kucan, 2013). This knowledge starts with a familiarity with the word and moves, as the language user is exposed to the word over many occasions, toward the ability to flexibly use it when speaking and writing. Our vocabulary development is never complete; in fact, we continue to learn new words throughout life. For many students, including many ELs, underdeveloped vocabulary knowledge represents a stumbling block to literacy development (August & Shanahan, 2006).

Whether we're listening or reading, we draw on these components of academic language as part of the meaning-making process (refer back to Figure

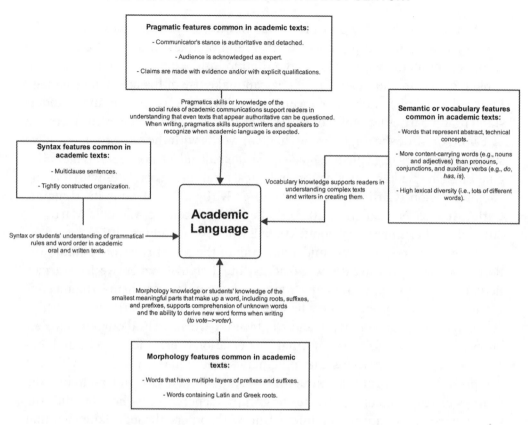

FIGURE 2.3. Components of academic language.

2.1 for a summary). As shown in Figure 2.3, we highlight some of the ways that these elements manifest themselves in academic texts and talk.

Content and Conceptual Knowledge

Wearing uniforms goes back many generations. Before we started this work on the uniform policy, I knew that my grandfather and his brothers and sisters had to wear a uniform at their church school. But now I also know that sometimes uniforms have been to show that the student goes to a prep school. I also know that today one of the reasons for uniforms is to show that everyone is the same. That we're all equal.

—SHAWN, fifth grader

In studying the school uniform policy, Shawn and his peers are bumping up against some big ideas and abstract concepts: equity, segregation, symbols, and representation. One of our most pressing issues today on the path to promoting advanced literacies among linguistically diverse populations is to increase our emphasis on knowledge building; we need to bring the world to students in meaningful ways, while supporting them to develop the foundational knowledge—content and conceptual—that they need in order to access and generate a range of texts, and to participate in communities engaged in literate activities, whether in the academic setting or workplace, now and as they grow up. Shawn knew a bit about uniforms before the unit began and so he was able to draw on some *existing conceptual knowledge*, but he has also been challenged to rethink his perspective as he has encountered, in the articles the class has read, persuasive arguments and new ideas about how clothing can serve to unite and divide groups.

For many decades, reading instruction was guided by the notion that if we just taught children how to read the words on the page, then the print would unlock the world for the reader (Compton et al., 2014). The reader would learn all about the world from print. This was and is the case for a small population of our students—our readers with a lot of knowledge about the world and the well-developed vocabulary needed to discuss this knowledge. Today's linguistically diverse population, and many of their peers, however, confirms that we really only learn from text when we are already quite familiar with what's on the printed page. A reader's comprehension of a story depends greatly upon the knowledge and language he or she brings to the experience. And a writer's ability to communicate his or her ideas and reach his or her audience depends greatly upon the knowledge and language he or she has to draw on. If our students are to learn through text and to develop their advanced literacies, then we need to focus on building up their knowledge of many of the concepts, ideas, and information that go into this thing we call "world knowledge." At the same time, when we cultivate conceptual and content knowledge among our students we build strong oral and written language skills—and vice versa; after all, big ideas and complex questions cannot be separated from the language used to represent them. But there is reason to think carefully about why we need to privilege the knowledge-building aspect of our instruction, even when we're focusing on language.

A recent study by Arya, Hiebert, and Pearson (2011) sheds light on the important role that background knowledge plays in reading comprehension. In a study with upper elementary students, the authors examined the extent of the impact that *text-level factors*, such as the types of words used in the text and the complexity of the sentences, and *reader factors*, including background knowledge, had on students' comprehension of science texts. The science texts students read spanned a continuum from very familiar topics (jellybeans and toothpaste) to topics that were less familiar to most of the students (frogs and soil composition). Before they conducted the study, the authors expected that the complexity of the sentences in the text—whether, for example, they contained multiple prepositions, embedded clauses or adjectives—would be the crucial factor in explaining students' performances. But this was not what they found. Instead, they found that *when the topic was familiar* complexity of the sentences played only a minimal role in readers' comprehension of the texts. Simply put, readers knew much more about jellybeans and toothpaste—everyday objects—and this mattered most for how they made sense of what they read.

Critical Interpretation Skills

It seems like, in what we've read, that there is no answer about if it's good or bad to have school uniforms. At first I thought it was going to be good to have uniforms, but then the newspaper article made a case against it. That might have something to do with the author because he had to wear a uniform when he was growing up. I think when the principal decides whether or not we should wear uniforms starting next year, he should maybe remember that time we made decision about whether we should not have any sodas in our school anymore. Maybe he could use that [same process] for making the decision and weighing out the positives and negatives.

—MAYA, eighth grader

In this eighth-grade Rosa Parks School classroom, Maya is clearly showing signs of understanding how to work with information in the academic context, for the purpose of advanced literacies—in this case, a debate about school uniforms. She is grappling with a question for which there is no clear answer and showing signs of understanding exactly that—many questions do not have a clear answer. Maya is also reasoning through how the principal might, ultimately, make the decision. In so doing, appropriately and encouragingly, she is drawing an analogy to a previous policy decision in the school.

As in the school uniform policy exercise at Rosa Parks, today we are often asking our students to evaluate information, to synthesize information across sources, and to draw their own conclusions (Fischer & Pruyne, 2003; Murphy, Wilkinson, Soter, Hennessey, & Alexander, 2009; Murphy, Rowe, Ramani, & Silverman, 2014). We ask them to engage in critical interpretations of what they read and hear. Beyond merely asking students to summarize what the author has said, we have increased the emphasis on having them "critically interpret" what they read; to assess the extent to which the information presented in a text is truthful, for example, or even to explain the motives of a character in a fictional story who may have little in common with the reader (Norris, Phillips, & Osborne, 2007).

To develop competency in critical interpretation demands a certain awareness of perspective. Students will at times need to examine their own perspectives or beliefs in relation to those presented in a text. At other times they
will need to understand or even situate themselves—if only temporarily—in
the shoes of the author (Barzilai & Eshet-Alkalai, 2015). We are just beginning in the field of literacy research to understand the very specific ways in
which this competency develops and supports academic reading and writing
(Vaughn et al., 2015). But research conducted in the last decade does show that
the developmental period from middle childhood through early adolescence is
one wherein there is a progression beyond perspective taking that is mostly
relegated to understanding relationships between peers and family. We refer to
perspective-taking skills that develop so that students are able to apply them
to social issues, such as racism or genocide (Selman, 2003), which bodes well
for the needed push toward studying complex ideas and issues (see Chapter 3
for more on this topic).

This composite competency also requires students to be able to hold information in mind and to engage in mental manipulation—as if holding a gem in
your hands and turning it to examine its many facets. We can think of these
as mental routines that we learn through engaging in them. Supporting our
students to see that there isn't a single, correct way to interpret a text or to
view an issue helps them to engage in the habits of mind that are common in
all knowledge-building fields (Moje, 2007; Qian & Alvermann, 2000).

Argumentation

I disagree with Jim because . . . well, because the way I have been thinking
about these issues of equity and fairness is that we have a right to self-
expression. Based on the research our group did, we don't think there is
enough evidence to decide that our clothing is a distraction and make a policy.
                                                              —RAFAEL, sixth grader

Rafael is in the middle of his presentation as part of the unit taking up the
question of school uniforms. It is clear that he is integrating his knowledge
gained from the articles he has read with his developing understanding of
persuasive rhetoric. While he may falter somewhat in developing the first line
of his argument about equity, fairness, and self-expression, he is doing some
clear, informed critical thinking—the foundation for a strong argument. Students require argumentation skills to create logical, stepwise arguments to justify their perspectives to others. These skills are often present in the youngest
of children (we've all had the experience of negotiating with a preschooler!),

but require additional polishing in academic settings where the definition of a "persuasive argument" differs from that which dominates day-to-day conversation.

In academic settings, a persuasive argument often begins by acknowledging the opponent's argument and then proceeding to systematically disprove it with pieces of evidence drawn from reliable sources. In the successful argument, the speaker positions him- or herself as somewhat emotionally detached from the argument and as more authoritative (e.g., using phrases like "The vast number of available studies suggest . . ." instead of "I think most studies suggest . . ."). In contrast, in our everyday conversational contexts, successful argumentation tends to follow a much less systematic structure and is often based on the level of passion that the speaker brings. Unlike the situation in which the timer is on for a formal debate or we're writing a letter to the mayor, during persuasive argument in our household or on the street corner in our community, we might repeat ourselves, go off on a tangent, bring in an anecdote that plays to the person we're speaking with, and even plead emotionally for understanding.

Once he has built up enough knowledge about the topic, generally, the challenge for a student like Rafael during the school uniform debate work is twofold: he must read, comprehend and select appropriate evidence to support his argument and he must package this argument and its accompanying evidence using language that his audience will find persuasive. Often this exercise requires students to reflect on multiple texts—some that contain conflicting arguments, a skill known as "multiple document literacy" (Anmarkrud, Bråten, & Strømsø, 2014).

Looking Ahead: Leading Advanced Literacies Instruction to Promote Four Key Competencies

Getting to advanced literacies among our linguistically diverse learners means, in most schools with large numbers of these students, a different instructional approach altogether. We therefore think of the component skills as *necessary but not sufficient to* support students in acquiring knowledge from text and producing the sophisticated oral and written language associated with advanced literacies. Yet unlike instruction that builds component skills, there is not a finite set of facts or concepts to be learned to get to the composite competencies and therefore advanced literacies; these are flexible competencies that support us in acquiring and sharing knowledge of the world, even as what counts as "knowledge" continues to rapidly evolve. That is, in this domain of advanced literacies, the component skills are much more mastery-oriented than the composite competencies are. For example, there are 26 letters and approximately 44 sounds and students can attain mastery, usually around third grade, in putting those together—whether for word reading or spelling. In contrast, composite skills are always evolving for each of us, based on our interactions with print, and as our literacy-based society evolves.

At the same time, evidence suggests that we don't spend much time teaching these advanced literacies competencies. Therefore, reimagining classrooms, including content-area classrooms, as sites for the development of advanced literacies for a sizable—and rapidly growing—population of linguistically diverse students, including ELs and students who have had fewer opportunities to be exposed to the academic English used at school, will demand significant time, effort, and change.

Supporting advanced literacies instruction demands that leaders focus on four aspects within their schools: (1) the quality of the day-to-day instruction that students receive; (2) the degree to which learning is coherent and cohesive as a result of using a shared platform for learning; (3) the manner in which assessment is used to identify the population's and individual learner's strengths and needs; and (4) the degree to which adult learners are provided with supportive and tailored professional learning. In the next chapter, we discuss each of these aspects in greater detail and the motivation for each as part of a comprehensive effort to promote advanced literacies.

As we continue to ask students to read and write for a host of purposes, there are important ways that we can and should support all students to develop these skills. The only way to do this is to spend more time building their oral and written language skills—developing their specialized knowledge about language and the world simultaneously. In the remaining chapters of this book, we dig deeply into what instruction to promote advanced literacies for all students looks like—ultimately supporting the instructional leader's shift to an instructional model that focuses much more explicitly on the relationship between language and advanced literacies tasks.

CHAPTER 3

Defining Instructional Leadership
for Advanced Literacies

Principal Lansdowne sat with her literacy leadership team poring over their students' state performance data from the prior academic year. The results were disappointing after an academic year in which numerous new programs and interventions had been introduced to support struggling students, even as faculty and staff attended many days of literacy-focused professional learning. The leadership team knew that action was needed if they were going to foster advanced literacies in their students, a concept their principal had introduced as a top priority for the coming year. The challenge, however, was that no one around the table was entirely sure what to adjust in their existing model to best fulfill their ambitious mission. They had, indeed, tried so many different initiatives and programs already.

For school leaders today, preparing students for 21st-century literacy demands means shifting to a 21st-century instructional model—and intentionally leaving some of our traditional approaches and practices behind. This 21st-century model hinges on high-quality instruction and literacy-learning opportunities, *each* day, *all* day, in *every* classroom, whether in the elementary or the middle school. In other words, to achieve advanced literacies for all, especially in settings characterized by linguistic diversity, leaders must work to create a cohesive literacy environment across the building. Doing so requires a strategic plan that puts the school's focus and energy into daily literacy-learning opportunities afforded to all students. The plan's elements would be there to prevent difficulties, augment skills and competencies, and ensure more consistency and cohesion for students and teachers alike. Built into it would be a model of professional development that reflects what we know about 21st-century adult learning.

How is this different from decades past? Well, over the years, in an effort to improve literacy rates, we have engaged in a number of very specific initiatives and practices, limited to certain groups, formats, and foci that we now know are insufficient: we have helped individual educators to plan and design their lessons, supported them with model units to guide them in the subsequent design of their own units, trained them on programs and supports for struggling readers, and provided them with guidance on how to meet the latest set of literacy standards based on students' test scores. We have held 1-day workshops and trainings to build knowledge of the latest practices and strategies to boost classroom quality and outcomes. We have relied on the literacy block to teach reading and writing almost exclusively in the primary grades. And lastly, we have focused more on component skills than composite competencies.

We know now that this traditional approach—one that focuses on specific classrooms, teachers, skills, and initiatives—does not and will not "add up" to the universal gains in language and literacy, and therefore content learning, that we need to see in many more of our students if they are to be successful in today's knowledge-based economy and society. Just as the field has pushed for the move from chalkboards to smart boards, from notepads to iPads, and from encyclopedia sets to encyclopedia websites, we also need to bring structural and process-driven change that is research-driven to our everyday approach to literacy learning and instruction.

As with any change effort, many potential starting places would seem to hold promise. However, based on our own experience and the research on literacy improvement, we have identified *four key shifts* (see Figure 3.1) that are crucial for supporting progress toward advanced literacies for all, thinking especially about settings serving large numbers of linguistically diverse learners. Together, these shifts focus on (1) strengthening day-to-day instructional practices (i.e., the instructional core); (2) sharpening the role that student data play in our improvement efforts; (3) ensuring the presence of high-quality plans and curricular materials in use in all classrooms; and (4) guaranteeing that the professional learning provided to educators is high quality. *Why these four shifts, in particular?* The reason is that they are interconnected and are what the field widely considers to be high-impact levers, foundational to any 21st-century literacy model (Paine, 2004; Torgeson, Houston, & Rissman, 2007). Without any one of these, the effort toward promoting advanced literacies for all will be compromised; they are the cornerstones of a cohesive model.

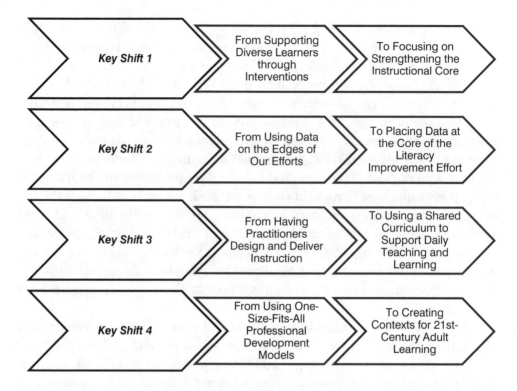

FIGURE 3.1. Key shifts for promoting advanced literacy instruction.

Organization of This Chapter

In this chapter, we provide an overview of leading advanced literacies instruction characterized by these shifts before discussing implementation of each shift in Chapters 4–7, respectively. Here, we describe each one in brief and provide its rationale, in the context of today's literacy demands. For each, we also discuss the understandings and assumptions that guide the traditional approach still in place at many school sites—arguably 20th-century rather than 21st-century ones. We present the change in mind-set that leaders must adopt in order to match today's context, to ensure that literacy instruction is not guided by a set of outdated understandings about learners and/or theories of learning and teaching. Finally, we close the chapter with the goal of supporting the school leader in laying the groundwork for buy-in and participation in what will be a significant change process. We well appreciate that this change process can be difficult for individuals, and that it therefore demands a systemic, inclusive approach.

So, to begin to implement these shifts at school sites, we suggest three action steps for leaders carrying out this work. *Action Step 1* involves creating a school-based literacy team, which includes the school-level leader in charge of the effort, to ensure distributed leadership and an inclusive improvement effort, preconditions for successful sustained change. *Action Step 2* involves taking an inventory of the current state of a school site's instructional model as it maps on to the four shifts: the curricular programs, assessments, interventions, and adult learning context. After all, any reform process starts with careful planning and a shared understanding of the starting point, including areas of strength and areas needing improvement. *Action Step 3* supports the school leader in working with the literacy team to generate an advanced literacies mission statement to guide their efforts.

Key Shift 1: From Supporting Diverse Learners through Interventions to Focusing on Strengthening the Instructional Core

The instructional core, the particulars of day-to-day instruction, is the bread and butter of any educational system. Our learners spend up to 20 hours per week engaged with the instructional core and what it has to offer. For this reason, it's also where our efforts to improve literacy rates can have the most impact. But there is a somewhat troublesome history as to how we've thought about the instructional core with regard to boosting the literacy outcomes for all students, especially those who are academically vulnerable. For decades, when dealing with at-risk and struggling populations, we have turned to specific interventions and supplemental instruction as a remedy. And to be frank, for many schools, especially those serving large numbers of linguistically diverse learners struggling to master composite competencies, betting on interventions hasn't worked.

We know that the development of advanced literacies and its associated competencies are cumulative and require multiple exposures. In most cases, supplemental interventions fall short on two counts:

1. They lack the intensity of exposure needed to develop the competencies, especially composite ones, that are needed to read, communicate, and reason in today's postsecondary and professional contexts. We know that these skills are best taught as part of everyday instruction, within heterogeneous settings, and while moving across domains (reading, writing, listening, and speaking).
2. By design, interventions are most useful to address a weakness in a very specific skill—one that can be easily targeted through repetition and generally lends itself to mastery, such as word-reading accuracy.

The unsuitability of intervention-based remedies only seems to increase with societal changes. The characteristics of today's learner population and the magnitude of the transformation in literacy skills and competencies required reinforces our need for a much more universal approach to providing targeted instruction. Figure 3.2 provides a summary of this changing context. Take, for example, the issues of meeting the needs of linguistically diverse students. In many schools serving high numbers of linguistically diverse students, in fact, the ELs and their peers are more alike than different when it comes to their literacy learning needs (Lesaux & Kieffer, 2010; Kieffer & Vukovic, 2012). In our own research with sixth-grade readers enrolled in 26 classrooms in a large, urban district, we observed common sources of difficulty for strug-gling readers from non-English-speaking homes and those from English-only households. Thinking back to Chapter 2 and our composite competencies in the advanced literacies domain, academic vocabulary knowledge was signifi-cantly underdeveloped for both groups, who consistently demonstrated read-ing comprehension abilities well below the national average.

Outdated Guiding Assumptions and Principles	21st-Century Realities and Guiding Principles

• Students learning academic English at school represent a small subpopulation of learners.
 	
• The strengths and needs of ELs and their classmates are distinct and necessarily demand different approaches.
 	
• The instructional core is preparing the majority of students to engage in advanced literacies tasks.
  ▪ Therefore, those who struggle need supplemental intervention.
	• The school-age population is linguistically diverse. There are 400+ native languages in the United States and in many districts, ELs represent the majority.
	  ▪ By 2030, 40% of the school-age population in the United States will speak a language other than English at home.
	
	• In many classrooms, the literacy strengths and needs of ELs and their English-only peers are more similar than they are different. Learning academic English, oral and written, should be an instructional priority for all.
	
	• In many settings, the instructional core needs to be updated and upgraded to match student needs and today's literacy demands.
	  ▪ When large numbers of students are struggling, the core should first be adjusted as the primary line of defense and response.

FIGURE 3.2. Capturing the context of Key Shift 1.

Moving beyond underdeveloped academic vocabulary, we've found that students from English-only homes as well as ELs also struggle to understand the features of academic language—the sentence structures, text organization patterns, and common academic words and phrases (e.g., *therefore, as a result*) that are found in textbooks and other academic texts (Uccelli et al., 2015). It is not that our ELs are not poised to learn; the learning growth rates for many are on par with the national average. Instead, we can think of the underperformance of these students at scale as a symptom of the mismatch between the intensity of our instruction—the extent to which we focus on developing language and knowledge as two competencies that underlie successful reading comprehension—and our students' needs. Using interventions to support these learners represents one area of incompatibility between our instructional model and our students' needs (Francis et al., 2006).

As a caveat, this is not to suggest that ELs, especially those in the early stages of English language learning, do not require targeted instruction to support their English language development. If that's the case, however, we cannot count this as a literacy intervention. Furthermore, those students with identified learning differences require intensive research-based interventions, especially to bolster component skills. In schools where a high-quality core is in place, this is a small group. Students identified as both ELs and as having learning differences (estimated to be about 8% of the EL population) require services to support both English language development and literacy skills (National Center for Educational Statistics, 2009; Peña, Bedore, & Gillam, 2011; Rodriguez, Carrasquillo, & Lee, 2014). These are ELs who, when compared to "true peers" (students with similar language proficiency levels and experiencing similar opportunities to acquire English), are demonstrating distinct difficulties and acquiring English literacy skills at a significantly slower pace (Brown & Doolittle, 2008). And, yet, these additional supports should still always take place against the backdrop of a strong instructional core, serving to reinforce what students are learning each day and to help them to better access the core curriculum.

In summary, as shown in Figure 3.3, shifting the focus from supplemental interventions to the instructional core will begin to address some key problems facing educators today: high rates of referrals to special education services and overrepresentation of certain groups within the special education system (Harry & Klingner, 2014); the challenges and costs associated with providing supplemental interventions, often ineffective; and the low literacy skills among the overall population, including those high school graduates who need remediation at college and those college graduates who don't have the technical literacy skills to match workplace demands (Organization for Economic Cooperation and Development, 2010).

Problems to Be Addressed by Key Shift 1	Target Outcomes (see Chapter 4)
• Low literacy rates among the overall population, but especially among subgroups (e.g., ELs). • The rising costs of interventions and difficulty staffing supplemental interventions. • Disappointment over the often negligible effects interventions have on students' skills and competencies. • High rates of referral to special education.	• Site-based selection of a set of schoolwide instructional practices and routines for implementation. • Successful implementation of those high-level instructional practices and routines across classrooms. • Reduction in the number of students who need intervention. • Reduction in the amount of money spent on interventions. • Decreases in the numbers of students referred to special education.

FIGURE 3.3. Key Shift 1: Theory of change.

The task, then, that leaders face is the reimagination of the instructional core to build advanced literacies for all. In Chapter 4, we provide support to the reader to lead the implementation of a shift from focusing on supplemental interventions to a site-based, deep, sustained focus on improving the instructional core.

Key Shift 2: From Using Data on the Edges of Our Efforts to Placing Data at the Core of the Literacy Improvement Effort

As in many fields, effective educational practice starts with data. Yet one of the greatest missed opportunities in schools today has to do with how data are used in our improvement efforts. We can all agree that we have more data on our students than ever before, and in many cases too much data to be useful. But in most schools our team has worked with, we find that data are not actually central to the overall literacy improvement efforts. To be sure, a school population's test scores might drive a sense of urgency, even panic, about needed action. For example, we might hear instructional leaders and teachers enumerating percentages of learners who scored at low levels, and in what areas, on a state assessment. Most often, assessment results are central to a case conference about a struggling student, in large part due to compliance with policy. This is also the context in which we tend to be most comfortable with data, looking very closely at an individual's performance and profile. We might even group all of the students who performed at a certain level on a state end-of-year assessment for intervention. Figure 3.4 provides a summary of this context.

But there is a missing piece that lies between looking at school-level literacy rates and digging into a single struggling reader's profile—and that missing piece must be addressed if we are to get to providing advanced literacies for all. *What is it?* Well, rarely, if ever, at school sites do we hear analysis and discussion of patterns and trends in the data by specific literacy component skill across classrooms and grades. These discussions focused on instructional trends and patterns are central, though, because they support the differentiation of the instructional core (i.e., the lessons *all* students receive in the literacy block). While we have tended to think of differentiation as being about individual learners, differentiation is primarily about molding our teaching routines and curriculum to support and challenge all of our learners (Kovaleski & Pederson, 2008). Although paramount to meeting students' needs, differentiating the core of instruction is often an overlooked step in instructional planning.

The individual's needs are important, to be sure; for that reason, when looking at student test scores, the first impulse many of us have is to look at individual students. We want to see how each student performed, and to try

Outdated Guiding Assumptions and Principles	21st-Century Realities and Guiding Principles
• State assessment data inform our understanding of individual readers. • Assessment data that show student difficulties signal the need for supplemental intervention(s). • Large-scale assessment performance levels ("proficient," "warning") or scores on global assessments provide key information for grouping for literacy interventions.	• State assessment data are most soundly used to understand population-level trends and patterns in student performance and to evaluate the quality of our programs. • Assessment data that show student difficulties often signal the need for adjustments to the instructional core. • Because many assessments tap composite competencies, rather than component skills, these data are not specific enough to match student needs to interventions.

FIGURE 3.4. Capturing the context of Key Shift 2.

to gain a fine-grained understanding of specific difficulties. But more often than not, when we became too focused on individual students we are overlooking the way in which the needs of that individual connect to the needs of classmates and peers. In most instances, because the individual's needs mirror those of the larger population, an adjustment to the core is in fact a better starting place than going straight to intervention.

This is particularly the case in our partner large urban district; students' shared backgrounds—in this case, the large and growing population of linguistically diverse learners—shape students' needs, resulting in some collective strengths and instructional mandates. What these data often suggest is that the instruction is failing to meet most ELs' needs, with the majority showing little progress. This is a clear sign that the instructional core must be adjusted. In fact, many ELs are taught in what have been dubbed "disabling contexts," classrooms with too few opportunities to acquire language and literacy skills or to receive instruction that is tailored to their needs (Orosco & Klingner, 2010).

A Cautionary Tale: Why Focusing on Test Item Types Is Not the Same as Differentiating the Core for Advanced Literacies

We can't just use any data to strengthen the instructional core; this can be a very problematic exercise if we are using the wrong type of data to inform our decisions. In many schools, we hear instructional leaders and teachers talking about the need for more instruction around "main ideas" and more work on "summarizing" because those were the question types on last year's test that posed the greatest difficulty to students. We must recall, however, that identifying a main idea is an advanced literacy composite competency. Many different skills—reading comprehension skills, knowledge of the purpose for reading, and the ability to use language to craft a concise summary—support students in summarizing a text. To many school leaders, it might seem that directing instructional attention to teaching "main idea" or "summarizing" in response to the state test results means that the core is being differentiated to match learners' needs and to promote their literacy skills. Why is this not the case? Well, item-level data give us the "what" but not the "why." That is, we don't actually know the source of literacy difficulty or weakness that is driving these unfortunate test results. As a result, our instructional response is often inefficient and ineffective.

Let's play out an example. Take the authors of this book and let's imagine that each one struggled with the test items on last spring's end-of-year state test that would be considered an assessment of "finding the main idea." Nonie might have struggled because she doesn't read the words with enough accuracy and fluency to focus on meaning making while reading. She is one of a small number of students in her classroom who has not responded to the high-quality phonics instruction provided as part of the core, and who is demonstrating signs of a learning difference (Nelson, Benner, & Gonzalez, 2003). Emily might have struggled with that question because she is still gaining command of the academic English used in print. She may be an EL or be an English-only student who has simply not had the opportunity to acquire this language. And Sky might have had sufficient word-reading and academic English skills, but may not have had sufficient background knowledge of the passage's topic. Despite these differences, the end result was the same for us all. Be that as it may, more instruction in "finding the main idea" for each is unlikely to be the best use of time; in Nonie's case it most certainly isn't if this is the extent and focus of her supplemental intervention.

In summary, as discussed in Key Shift 1, the classrooms in our schools work best and serve the greatest number of students when there is a strong core of instruction. Getting to this strong core means adapting the general guidance provided by curriculum and in standards to fit the needs and strengths demonstrated by a particular group of learners. After all, many curricula are not designed for ELs and other linguistically diverse students; they focus on teaching reading and writing skills, and assume that most students have

Problems to Be Addressed by Key Shift 2	Target Outcomes (see Chapter 5)
• Inefficient, often frustrating or overwhelming, data analysis because data are in multiple places. • Time-consuming data analyses because of the primary focus on looking at each individual. • Faculty feel that programs, interventions, and tireless efforts are "not working."	• Site-level discussions and planning on population trends and patterns of performance in data. • Reduction in the amount of time spent examining individuals' assessment results. • Reduction in literacy-related difficulties because instructional core has been tailored to reflect the needs of most students. • Rapid growth in the skills targeted by the intervention due to a closer match between the students' needs and the intervention.

FIGURE 3.5. Key Shift 2: Theory of change.

already acquired the prerequisite oral language needed to access the planned classroom texts and talk (Klingner & Eppolito, 2014). This is not always the case for linguistically diverse learners. Therefore, a first imperative step in analyzing student data is to identify the overall needs of the learners in our classrooms—to understand the emerging literacy skills and competencies and identify what these patterns and trends mean for daily instruction. Described in further detail in Chapter 5, doing so demands at least two crucial strategies: (1) to organize school-level data in a manner that allows instructional leaders and teachers to easily observe patterns and trends in order to design and deliver a differentiated instructional core; and (2) to carry out follow-up assessment to identify the specific literacy skills and competencies that are the sources of the weakness or breakdown among our learners who are struggling. Figure 3.5 summarizes the changes in Key Shift 2.

Key Shift 3: From Having Practitioners Design and Deliver Instruction to Using a Shared Curriculum to Support Daily Teaching and Learning

Educators need clear steps and quality materials to create a literacy-enriched learning environment that is at once structured, interactive, and engaging. At the same time, teachers cannot design *and* deliver the highest quality literacy instruction day after day, and month after month, throughout the school year. Knowledge- and language-building literacy instruction—the kind of instruction that all students deserve and require—cannot be achieved at scale if teachers are expected to provide these learning opportunities by drawing from sets of disconnected resources and materials. When provided with too many documents and plans, and even too many resources, while lacking a single, clear standards-based curriculum to follow, and short on time to design curricula, the teacher will experience direction that is often more demanding than supportive. Meanwhile, the student experience is more disjointed than it is cohesive. Teachers scramble to *create and deliver daily plans* rather than to focus on their students' learning needs. We acknowledge that when educators are provided with resources that require them to pick and choose from various curricula, there will be teachers who bring the experience and expertise it takes to cultivate the very best of learning environments. We cannot expect, however, that *all* teachers will bring this experience and expertise to the classroom. At scale, this becomes a matter of equity for students and for teachers, who are differentially provided with the resources they need to experience success in the classroom.

Therefore, a key mechanism for creating high-quality literacy learning environments is a coordinated approach to the curriculum, one that provides educators with a single, shared platform, in the form of a core reading curriculum, for meeting readers' needs across grades. Beyond the instructional benefits, when a high-quality core literacy curriculum is implemented with fidelity,[1] there are benefits to the classroom and school environment: effective classroom management practices (e.g., behavior and time management); developmentally appropriate pacing that promotes student engagement and on-task behaviors; and literacy-rich materials (libraries, posters, props, etc.) that are familiar to teachers and readers, and that support a cohesive classroom experience. Finally, when coupled with the right professional development model (see Key Shift 4), it is a key mechanism for buffering the effects of, and beginning to reduce, teacher turnover. Figure 3.6 summarizes this context.

Outdated Guiding Assumptions and Principles	21st-Century Realities and Guiding Principles
• Educators have enough time during the instructional day and during their planning time to find high-quality materials and design lessons that add up to a long-term plan for learning. • Curriculum is not a teaching support. • Curriculum deprofessionalizes teaching. • Standard training and professional development has supported teachers to be able to design curriculum.	• The little planning time that teachers do have should be spent focusing on planning for the implementation of differentiated instruction. • Having a well-designed, high-quality core curriculum in place acknowledges the teacher's primary role as an expert in instructional delivery. • Research demonstrates that a high-quality curriculum is a professional tool that contributes to daily on-the-job learning. ▪ Promotes subject-matter knowledge and content-based pedagogical knowledge. ▪ Many teachers struggle to design a high-quality, aligned curriculum to promote knowledge-based literacy development across the year.

FIGURE 3.6. Capturing the context of Key Shift 3.

---

[1] Sometimes, "fidelity" to the curriculum is interpreted as an almost dogmatic adherence to what is written on the page, even if all signs indicate that the instruction is not working. This is not how we define fidelity. Instead, fidelity refers to the delivery of instruction that is first presented as written and then is systematically and carefully tailored to the needs of the student population by a team of educators. As a result, the instruction provided is the same in all classrooms where the curriculum is being used.

In our work over the last decade, we have repeatedly heard teachers explaining their frustration with the amount of time they spend locating texts and other materials, leaving them little time for designing *how* to deliver this content. Yet in schools serving linguistically diverse learner populations, there is often much work to be done in differentiating the delivery of the instruction to meet the needs of students. If we have not engineered the school day to allow for the collaborative and time-intensive endeavor of designing curriculum, then we cannot assume that educators are properly supported to do this work in addition to delivering instruction. Thus, in contrast to viewing curriculum as a mechanism for deprofessionalizing the work of teachers, we view offering a well-designed core curriculum as a way in which leaders can acknowledge the teacher's primary role as expert in instructional delivery, by providing him or her with the tools necessary to enact this role.

High-quality curriculum materials designed to promote student learning and teacher learning are what Davis and Krajcik (2005) have referred to as "educative." By presenting teachers with activities and content that represent best practices, the materials can bolster a teacher's subject matter knowledge, pedagogical content knowledge (e.g., how to teach vocabulary and support discussions), and pedagogical content knowledge for disciplinary practices (e.g., how to teach the scientific method). In other words, the curriculum can become a tool for powerful daily on-the-job training.

In summary, as shown in Figure 3.7, implementing a core curriculum— either packaged or designed locally under specific circumstances—is a key

Problems to Be Addressed by Key Shift 3	Target Outcomes

• Students' content-based learning opportunities are variable and inconsistent.
  ▪ Little alignment from classroom to classroom and from grade to grade.
 	
• Teachers don't have enough high-quality instructional materials.
 	
• On-boarding process for new teachers is limited and unsystematic due to lack of concrete tools.
	• Students' learning opportunities are more consistent and cohesive from classroom to classroom and from grade to grade.
	
	• Teachers feel more supported with respect to availability of teaching tools.
	
	• There is a shared language at the site around instructional content and routines.
	  ▪ Supports more specific conversations about differentiated approach to the instructional core.
	
	• Curriculum is a key mechanism for on-boarding new faculty; supports smooth transition.

FIGURE 3.7. Key Shift 3: Theory of action.

strategy to getting to advanced literacies for all. For students, it means curricular coherence across the day and the whole school year; and for adults, it means a shared language for teaching and learning at the site, which is basic to the overall literacy reform effort. Educators, like all professionals, require a very strong platform to work from. In Chapter 6 we focus on leading the implementation of a shared platform for teaching and learning, which starts with a careful curricular selection and/or design process.

Key Shift 4: From Using One-Size-Fits-All Professional Development Models to Creating Contexts for 21st-Century Adult Learning

Adults in our schools powerfully influence students' language and reading development; after all, knowledge is not institutionalized—and excellence resides in the individuals in the organization. These individuals are the key mechanisms through which services, supports, and interventions promote development and learning. This is especially true for teachers of ELs, who are most often acquiring the skills to be linguistically responsive *in vivo*, that is, in real time, because of little formal training provided before they enter the classroom. Yet one's professional success and impact depends directly upon training and continuing education, and many educators are not provided with sufficient or effective training opportunities to deliver on this promise. For some, there is no training at all; for others, the professional education lacks sufficient intensity and relevance to gain traction in the practice setting.

That is, even when professional development does occur, our current paradigm favors periodic training sessions that are relatively brief, one-size-fits-all, and disconnected from daily practice. But we've learned over the years that this traditional model of professional development actually has minimal impact on reforming practice—and certainly won't get us to advanced literacies for all. This means, for example, that regardless of the number of professional development points any given teacher accumulates, his or her instructional approaches tend not to change and his or her students' opportunities to learn tend to remain static. This professional development model is often ineffective because it is conducted outside of meaningful contexts, guided by topics and approaches that often reflect educational fads. The trainings are also typically short in duration (e.g., one-half or full day) and maintain teacher isolation by having individuals participate alone rather than as school-based teams, and consequently lack intensity as well as authenticity. Figure 3.8 provides a summary of this context.

Outdated Guiding Principles and Practices	21st-Century Realities and Guiding Principles

• Specific topics of professional interest (e.g., strategies for teaching ELs; leading discussions in the upper elementary classroom) addressed independently will support improved practice in advanced literacies.
 	
• Brief, one-off sessions transform educator knowledge and practice about instruction to promote advanced literacies.
 	
• Individual teachers sign up for outside sessions based on their own interest(s) and professional needs—or their participation is mandated.
	• To promote advanced literacies for all, professional learning opportunities need to have these characteristics:
	  ■ Focused on a limited set of pedagogical strategies and approaches to build composite competencies (see Chapters 2 and 4), anchored in a knowledge-building plan for students and teachers.
	  ■ Continuous, site-based work guided and refined on the basis of data (both student data and teacher data collected via observations).
	  ■ Involves site-based teams made up of educators and instructional leaders with decision-making authority.
	  ■ Opportunities for feedback on teaching and guided reflection on practice.
	
	• If off-site professional learning occurs, it is coupled with planned site-based follow-up and opportunities for classroom-based application and feedback.
	  ■ Note: Off-site professional development offered by experts can be an excellent tool for launching a site-based initiative.

FIGURE 3.8. Capturing the context of Key Shift 4.

In any profession, the task of transforming knowledge, and therefore practice, cannot be understated. For teachers, the knowledge gained in professional learning is often challenging to put into practice upon return to the classroom because little opportunity for application can be provided in such short professional development sessions and coaching is rarely offered (Darling-Hammond, Wei, Andree, Richardson, & Orphanus, 2009). For example, some studies demonstrate that, on average, teachers require at least 20 separate instances of in-context practice—with scaffolding and support—before a new skill is mastered. And if the skill or competency being taught is more complex (such as composite competencies), the number of instances of practice required increases (Joyce & Showers, 2002). As with learning anything new, teachers often encounter difficulty when first introduced to a teaching technique. One finds that command only comes by persevering through these initially awkward, often frustrating attempts. Without support, most teachers will not persevere. Therefore, whether receiving professional development over a series of sessions or working in a professional learning community at their school sites, teachers need to be applying new learnings in their own classrooms. Finally, given this fact, effective professional development should be linked to a specific, site-level need as surfaced by data (Peery, 2004). This is particularly crucial for teachers of ELs and other linguistically diverse learners, who are rarely provided with professional support to create high-quality classrooms—ones where students are exposed to instruction that is understandable (sometimes called "comprehensible") and where explicit instruction is provided to foster academic language, oral language, and academic vocabulary development (Lucas, Villegas, & Freedson-Gonzalez, 2008; Ortiz & Artiles, 2010).

As shown in Figure 3.9, in schools where 21st-century adult learning is underway, a number of characteristics are clearly in evidence: we typically meet a highly collaborative staff that embraces a growth mind-set for themselves and for students—they are in the habit of ongoing practice and discussion about priority instructional techniques and problems. We find as well that challenges and professional development topics arise out of needs expressed by faculty or student data. In Chapter 7, we focus in detail on leading the process of creating the contexts—putting in place the structures and the processes—for 21st-century adult learning. If we are to get to advanced literacies for all, sustained approaches to effective staff development are a necessity.

Problems to Be Addressed by Shift 4	Target Outcomes

• Staff participate in general professional learning.
  ■ Often provides little opportunity for classroom-based application.
  ■ Faculty attend as individuals, not as part of a team focused on instructional improvement.
  ■ Topics are a list of "what's hot" in the field and based on district, not school, priorities.
	• A staff that embraces a growth mind-set and is guided by the principle that gaining command of new instructional strategies and knowledge takes time and requires ongoing practice.
	
	• There is distributed leadership among the staff around the literacy improvement effort. It is not tied to one person and is sustained in the face of turnover and absences.
	
	• Professional development plans arise out of needs expressed by faculty or student data.
	  ■ Strict adherence to subscribing only to those opportunities that are central to the improvement agenda.

FIGURE 3.9. Key Shift 4: Theory of action.

Laying the Groundwork for Advanced Literacy Leadership

As with any reform effort, identifying the *need* for change and committing to improvement is often the easy part. *Making it happen* is where the rubber hits the road. To that end, implementing and executing an effective change effort starts with laying the groundwork for buy-in and participation by all key players, followed by the identification of priorities. After all, we can't do everything at once, even if we know what needs to be done—we must take a staged approach and it must be politically wise. So, to begin to implement these shifts at school sites, we suggest three action steps.

Action Step 1: Create a Team

We suggest that leaders form a school-based literacy team comprised of individuals who represent a range of perspectives (classroom educators from across content areas, literacy and second-language learning specialists, and school leaders). This team, including the site-based instructional leader in charge of the literacy reform effort, would then move through two more action steps in order to identify priorities and immediate next steps.

Action Step 2: Conduct a Site-Based Inventory

As a second step, we suggest that the team take an inventory of the context of current literacy instruction: the curricular programs, data collection and use, interventions, and adult learning context. To take this inventory, team members together should work with the inventory provided (see the reproducible Leader's Tool 3.1 in the Appendix) to begin to identify areas of particular strength and areas for growth across the four shifts. Given that the model of advanced literacies leadership described here is a multistep and multiyear process, all shifts cannot be undertaken simultaneously. This inventory can support leaders in choosing which shifts to implement first, and in what progression. Then, the leaders and their team are referred to Chapters 4 to 7 for in-depth support in leading any one of those shifts.

Action Step 3: Drafting an Advanced Literacies Mission Statement at the Site

The final preparatory step involves generating an advanced literacies mission statement to guide the work at the site. This mission statement provides a single definition of what advanced literacies means at the site, one that all faculty can work from to design instruction. A mission statement serves to get everyone "on the same page" and to provide a touchstone that can be returned to through the course of implementation. Generating a mission statement is, again, the work of a larger representative team. An entire staff working first in small groups and then as a whole group can also generate a mission statement. What is of central importance is that multiple perspectives are represented. To support the drafting of a mission statement at any site, turn to the reproducible Leader's Tool 3.2 in the Appendix.

Summary and Next Steps

In this chapter, we presented the rationale for an approach to bolstering 21st-century advanced literacy teaching. We acknowledge that this involves shifts in how school leaders organize to support daily instruction, in the materials used to teach, in how struggling students are supported, and in how adult learning communities are designed. In the chapters that follow, we offer concrete guidance to leaders in making these shifts. In the next chapter, we tackle Key Shift 1.

PART II

Leading the Implementation of Four Key Site-Based Shifts for Progress

CHAPTER 4

Revisiting and Strengthening the Instructional Core

M oving classrooms, especially those serving linguistically diverse students, toward advanced literacies demands fundamental shifts in the way we view teaching and learning. Most importantly, we need to focus our attention on strengthening the instructional core, the first shift introduced in the previous chapter. The instructional core, which refers to the day-to-day instruction that all students receive, is rarely where we concentrate our efforts when faced with large numbers of struggling readers and writers; yet, this is where our students spend the majority of the school day *and* where our efforts to improve students' advanced literacies can have the most impact.

It can be appealing to address the needs of struggling readers through interventions that sit outside the core of instruction; by creating an elaborate menu of interventions, it *can feel* as if we are meeting the needs of each individual student at our school site. There is a sense of satisfaction in seeing the individualized attention intervention provides, but it is quite misplaced. The reality is that it simply does not work in today's schools. The schools we have worked with tend to place nearly all linguistically diverse students in literacy interventions. Typically, this is a response to data that suggest that most linguistically diverse students are not making progress, which is generally a symptom of an instructional core that does not meet their needs. In schools where these learners comprise the majority, the consequence is a literacy intervention system bursting at the seams, which is costly not only for a school's budget, but also in instructional time lost. Most importantly, and surprising as this may seem, interventions are rarely effective: they almost never result in increases in students' advanced literacies.

Why is intervention ineffective for building advanced literacies? Well, as shown in Figure 4.1, in part, this intervention-driven model for improvement fails because it is based on assumptions about learners and instruction that no longer hold true in most schools. But even in schools where these assumptions do hold true, interventions are still not the right mechanism for developing students' advanced literacies on the basis of their natural limitations.

First, they simply lack the intensity needed to develop 21st-century literacies. Let's keep in mind that advanced literacies are a constellation of competencies, for instance, the ability to synthesize information or to evaluate texts. These competencies require time to foster: students need repeated opportunities from classroom to classroom and across the school day to build these competencies. Interventions also have another limitation: one-on-one or small-group instruction focused on skill building that occurs outside of subject-area classrooms is a mismatch with what we know about the instructional conditions that foster advanced literacies competencies. Namely, students develop

Outdated Guiding Assumptions and Principles	21st-Century Realities and Guiding Principles

• Students learning academic English at school represent a small subpopulation of learners.
 	
• The strengths and needs of ELs and their classmates are distinct and necessarily demand different approaches.
 	
• The instructional core is preparing the majority of students to engage in advanced literacies tasks.
   ▪ Therefore, those who struggle need supplemental intervention.
	• The school-age population is linguistically diverse. There are 400+ native languages in the United States and in many districts, ELs represent the majority.
	   ▪ By 2030, 40% of the school-age population in the United States will speak a language other than English at home.
	
	• In many classrooms, the literacy strengths and needs of ELs and their English-only peers are more similar than they are different. Learning academic English, oral and written, should be an instructional priority for all.
	
	• In many settings, the instructional core needs to be updated and upgraded to match student needs and today's literacy demands.
	   ▪ When large numbers of students are struggling, the core should first be adjusted as the primary line of defense and response.

FIGURE 4.1. Capturing the context of Key Shift 1.

these competencies best when they have to use them for authentic purposes, like reading multiple texts to engage in a debate or to write a persuasive essay. Rather than target these skills through intervention, promoting advanced literacies must be an instructional goal shared by all teachers, who by adopting a common set of instructional practices—those documented to support linguistically diverse learners and to build advanced literacies for the 21st century—can achieve the coherence and cohesion that leads to a stronger core of instruction.

Hallmarks of Advanced Literacies Instruction

This context leads us to several questions: What is this common set of instructional practices? How are they different from what we've always done? How will we know when high-quality advanced literacies instruction is in place? In this chapter, we offer our answer to these questions by describing a set of high-impact instructional practices associated with students' development of advanced literacies. Incidentally, these are also the instructional practices that are often cited as supportive to ELs and nonmainstream English dialect speakers (August & Shanahan, 2006; Francis et al., 2006; Short & Fitzsimmons, 2007). In teaching to build advanced literacies *and* to support linguistically diverse learners, we are at the nexus of support and rigor, both meeting today's standards and responding to learner's needs. We refer to these as the *hallmarks of advanced literacies instruction*. Each of these hallmarks informs the design of reading, speaking/listening, and writing pedagogy as well as vocabulary teaching, as a crosscutting component of instruction for linguistically diverse students:

- *Hallmark 1:* Work with a variety of texts that feature big ideas and rich content.
- *Hallmark 2:* Talk/discuss to build language and knowledge.
- *Hallmark 3:* Use extended writing as a platform to build language and knowledge.
- *Hallmark 4:* Study a small set of high-utility vocabulary words needed to master language and content.
- *Hallmark 5:* Use schoolwide protocols to support reading, writing, speaking, and listening.

In addition to resulting in a more cohesive and contemporary (based on today's standards) learning experience for students, adopting the hallmarks supports faculty and leaders in developing a shared framework for their observation of teaching and planning instruction.

Organization of This Chapter

We begin this chapter by describing the substance of each of the five hallmarks and then outline the actions leaders can take to implement each at a school site. We note that these are not a restrictive set of instructional practices; instead our readers will find that there is much flexibility for designing an approach that reflects a state's or district's requirements and the particular needs of a site's student population. For instance, take our first hallmark. Because many districts have selected a set of grade-level texts or one textbook that students in each grade are required to read, actualizing this hallmark in instruction will often require the provision of more texts, some that contain additional richer content and some that are at different levels of readability.

Given that we view the hallmarks as a set of common instructional practices that should be used in all classrooms, we recommend that this work only take place after the first three action steps laid out in Chapter 3 have been undertaken, especially the crafting of an advanced literacies mission statement. These steps will build consensus around the hallmarks and identify areas where teachers will need extra support. Finally, we share a set of indicators in the form of an implementation checklist that leaders can use to gauge the site's baseline level of these (see Leader's Tool 4.1 in the Appendix).

The instructional model that is needed for 21st-century advanced literacies for all differs in striking ways from our traditional model. That is, historically, our grade-level instructional goals focused on teaching students content (dates, places of historical importance) or discrete skills (the ability to read 100 words per minute). These instructional goals—as well as the instructional practices used to achieve them—often differ from classroom to classroom and from content area to content area. In contrast, when schools adopt advanced literacies as a universal instructional end goal, they adopt a common set of instructional practices to be implemented in science, math, social studies, and English language arts—what we are referring to here as "the hallmarks" (see Figure 4.2).

In the sections that follow we describe each hallmark, laying out its substance and relevance to instruction. We then offer a short practice-based vignette from the Rosa Parks School that describes the particular hallmark in action. For each vignette, we provide the appropriate segment of our Leader's Tool 4.1, a checklist included that can be used to examine instruction for the

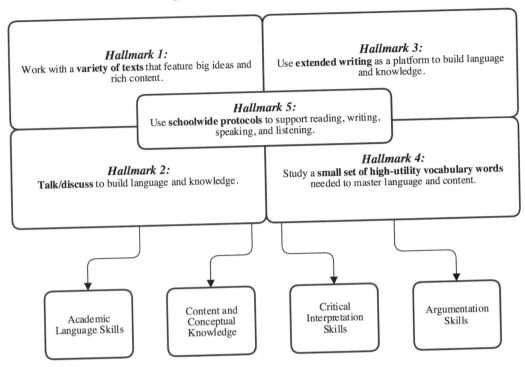

FIGURE 4.2. The hallmarks of advanced literacies instruction.

presence of the hallmarks at school sites (included in a reproducible form in the Appendix). For readers, the checklist can be paired with the vignette as an exercise in using the hallmarks as a set of "look-fors."

Hallmark 1: Work with a Variety of Texts That Feature Big Ideas and Rich Content

We have observed two practices around the role of text levels that need revisiting if schools are to get to advanced literacies for all. The first practice is that all texts used with linguistically diverse students are extremely challenging because they are at or above grade level (something that we see more and more as schools adopt standards-aligned curriculum) OR *all* texts are below grade level, offering little engaging content and compromising learning opportunities. Neither approach does much to move students' advanced literacies—in the first case, students can't engage in meaning making, and in the second, they are unlikely to grow their skills or knowledge nor maintain motivation and attention. To get past one or both of these problems, we advocate for the use of a variety of texts, sometimes referred to as "text sets." Each of these sets would include content-rich texts, but at the same time represent different levels of readability (Valencia, Wixson, & Pearson, 2014). The approach we have in mind pays less attention to a text's reading level (Lexile level) and more attention to questions like: What do students know that can help them to understand this text? How will the other texts we have read help students understand this text? After all, struggling readers can tackle grade-level texts when they have adequate background knowledge, which makes sets of texts on the same topic, some more complex and some less complex, a key support for linguistically diverse students on the path to consistently accessing grade-level texts with ease (Hiebert, 2013). In addition to printed texts, visual texts, such as photos and video, are important tools for literacy development.

Using a range of texts on a single topic—that is, our text sets—is also a good fit with our 21st-century focus on developing critical interpretation and argumentation skills, which depend upon adequate opportunities to reconcile texts that present different perspectives on an issue and/or that provide new information on a topic (Anmarkrud et al., 2014; Norris et al., 2008; Pressley & Afflerbach, 1995). We often advise starting with informational texts because they are filled with the complex, abstract, and sophisticated words (i.e., academic language) and the complex ideas that are part of the curriculum—and they often connect to real-world issues, which supports motivation and engagement (Baker et al., 2011). Combined with the appropriate instructional supports, text sets are an excellent and crucial starting place for building language and knowledge (Kieffer & Lesaux, 2007).

What Does 21st-Century Instruction with Engaging Texts Look Like?

Principal Lansdowne is observing a sixth-grade teacher, Michael Florence, as he prepares his students for a debate on the topic of U.S. immigration policy following the introduction of more stringent work visas, an issue that stands to impact many of his students' families. The class has been studying key U.S. immigration policies and has read six texts—two from national newspapers, two from the district-mandated textbook, and two from the *Time for Kids* magazine. In addition, they watched two evening news segments on the topic. The text set was assembled by members of the sixth-grade teaching team working with the school's reading specialist during one of two weekly planning periods provided to all grade-level teams.

In today's class, students are preparing for the debate by reviewing the texts in small groups and by drafting arguments for or against more restric-

INDICATORS OF HALLMARK 1 IN INSTRUCTION

Instructor communicates the purpose for reading the text in light of the unit's goals.	☑
Instructor connects the texts within the unit so that students understand the role that each text plays in building up their understanding of the unit topic.	☑
Instructor creates space for students to share alternative interpretations of the text.	☑
Instructor requires that students use text-based evidence to support any claims made about the text.	☑
Instructor creates opportunities for students to answer text-dependent questions through appropriately paced instruction that builds basic comprehension first, then moves to supporting readers in making inferences.	☑

tive immigration policies. Principal Lansdowne is impressed by the students' engagement with the texts. In small groups, students are busy rereading the texts and discussing the key pieces of evidence. It is obvious that Mr. Florence has worked hard to foster this engagement by creating an authentic purpose— the debate—for using the texts. He also began today's lesson by reviewing the purpose of each text in the text set—some were to build historical knowledge and others were chosen to build understanding of the current issues. Moving from group to group, Principal Lansdowne notices that there are multiple interpretations of many texts in the set—Felicia uses evidence from the text to argue that restricting immigration will lead to an increase in the number of jobs available, but Indira argues the opposite, also using text-based evidence. Principal Lansdowne knows that Mr. Florence will allow—in fact, support— these divergent interpretations as long as students provide evidence from the text to support their statements. To support struggling students, Mr. Florence walks from group to group posing text-based questions:

"Can you find the place in the text where the reporter summarizes his main argument?"
"What did the reporter say was the biggest reason why we should have more open immigration policies?"
"Can you find that statement in the text?"
"Why do you think the writer made that argument?"

Hallmark 2: Talk/Discuss to Build Language and Knowledge

We've all been in classrooms and observed typical classroom talk: a teacher asks a question, calls on a student to respond, the teacher then follows by evaluating the response (i.e., saying whether it's correct or incorrect)—and the interaction is complete. This common exchange is not going to get today's students to the levels of language and critical thinking that they are capable of—and that they need for academic and personal success. Getting past brief interactions and text for building language and knowledge and moving toward advanced literacies for all means using talk and discussion to develop both conversational and academic language and knowledge. In classrooms, this goal often translates into the use of project-based work that involves planning for extended discussion and talk: debates, speeches, presentations, and theater-based learning activities. These are learning tasks and activities where the central aim is to support students to *produce* academic language, through role play, collaboration, and research.

What's the benefit of producing more language? Well, for linguistically diverse learners, classroom academic talk simultaneously boosts knowledge of how to speak academic English and gives students a chance to be exposed to knowledge and perspectives that are challenging to access in texts (August, McCardle, & Shanahan, 2014; Coleman & Goldenberg, 2012; Vaughn et al., 2015). These interactions also give teachers a chance to informally assess ELs' burgeoning oral language skills (Francis et al., 2006). For nonmainstream dialect speakers, classroom talk is one of the best formats for helping students build awareness of how (and when) to shift language (what's called "metalinguistic awareness" or pragmatics; see Chapter 2) (Grosjean, 1998; Wolfram & Schilling-Estes, 2005). In fact, metalinguistic awareness has increasingly emerged in the literature as a crucial component of literacy success for speakers of African American English (AAE; Washington et al., 2013). Speaking AAE does *not* place children at risk for reading failure: many AAE speakers don't experience any reading difficulties. Instead it's low levels of *awareness and sensitivity to language* that appear to undermine students' success as readers (Terry & Connor, 2012; Washington et al., 2013). With this in mind, extended discussion and classroom talk emerges as a way to expose students to authentic opportunities to use academic language. In fact, in our own work, we've found that using talk to raise awareness of the features of academic language and to highlight when it should be used is one of the most important strategies in today's teaching toolkit (Galloway, Stude, & Uccelli, 2014).

To develop their language skills, ELs and linguistically diverse students need a lot of practice with language. In fact, the struggles that students encounter with producing academic language are very often linked with a lack of opportunity to participate in contexts where school-like language is used. Here, we are not just talking about ELs; many students require more opportunities for academic talk. Heath's (2012) ethnography, for instance, demonstrates the striking decrease over the last three decades in the amount of language that characterizes adolescents' daily life—across racial groups (African American and European American families) and socioeconomic backgrounds. For example, 14-year-olds today spend much less time engaged in back-and-forth conversations with adults at home: in 1979, the adolescents Heath studied spent about 89 minutes per afternoon engaged in this type of talk, but, by 2009, this had decreased to only 9 minutes. This positions the classroom as a critical site for increasing language production and learning for *all* adolescents.

And this can't be just about talk between teachers and students. Language also develops if there is extended back-and-forth discussion among students, organized around rich content and topics—and if we are going to get to genuinely language-rich environments, students are going to have to do much more of the talking. This is actually good news for teachers and students alike: beyond the cognitive and linguistic benefits, we know that extended talk and discussion creates a more engaging learning environment. For example, recent research shows us that fostering engagement by focusing on building student autonomy and collaboration produces greater gains in achievement (Guthrie, Wigfield, & You, 2012) and we know that talk-based learning tasks and projects can do exactly this. Also, because discussions that are text-based often center on negotiating the text's meaning, striving readers or students whose skills are emerging are able to struggle productively in a supported context (Aukerman, 2013).

What Does 21st-Century Discussion-Based Instruction Look Like?

Moving down the hall, Principal Lansdowne enters Rose Wong's fourth grade. Students there are discussing the text *The Skin I'm In* by Sharon Flake as well as a nonfiction text, *Middle School Confidential: Be Confident in Who You Are* by Annie Fox. The concept of "sibling rivalry" comes up as it relates to the characters in Flake's text; Ms. Wong asks students to interview their peers about their opinions. Students move between conversational language and

INDICATORS OF HALLMARK 2 IN INSTRUCTION

Instructor communicates the importance of using target words when speaking.	☑
Instructor acknowledges the challenges associated with learning new language and conveys an attitude that values experimenting with language by praising students' attempts at using target language when speaking (i.e., an expectation that students will *not* likely use words correctly or precisely at first).	☑
Instructor builds in talk routines if these are not already an integral part of the curriculum.	☑
Students are aware of talk routines and demonstrate a level of comfort with them.	☑
Student discussion is part of each lesson (e.g., short peer-to-peer interaction, debates, interviews).	☑
Students are encouraged to use peers as language resources when speaking (e.g., to build off of others' comments, to use words first introduced by other students).	☑
Students are asked to use previously taught words, language structures, and strategies for academic language learning when speaking.	☑

more academic language, with some students using a first language to share their ideas. Principal Lansdowne notes that Ms. Wong is moving throughout the room, listening intently to students, and encouraging attempts at using unfamiliar academic language—it's clear that she doesn't expect that students will use this language correctly or precisely at first and students are not uneasy with their attempts. Working explicitly with Juan and A'Lena, Ms. Wong scaffolds their academic language use by having them explain their thinking first by using conversational language and then by explaining the same thought using academic language. This kind of "code-switching" exercise is important and effective for building an understanding of language registers and use. Moving from group to group, Ms. Wong encourages students to use the language that peers provide to explain their thinking more clearly: "Marvin just said that 'sibling rivalry is very common.' That is a very accurate statement, using the word *common*, because *many* kids feel like they are competing with a sister or brother. We can all use Marvin's words when we speak and write." Students are familiar with accountable talk routines, as a set of discussion norms that the entire school has adopted, and Principal Lansdowne is pleased to hear familiar phrases that students have been taught ("I agree with you because . . ."; "Can you say more about that?"; "Where does it say that in the text? Can you show me?"). These talk routines appear in nearly every lesson, whether in the form of short think–pair–share interactions or extended debates, and it's starting to show in students' increased levels of comfort.

Hallmark 3: Use Extended Writing as a Platform to Build Language and Knowledge

Many writing assignments in today's schools are actually just brief writing "exercises"—on-demand writing (putting pencil to paper in a hurry), often in response to a prompt, and most often drawing on personal experience and opinion (sometimes referred to as "journal responses" or "free writes") (Lawrence, Galloway, Yim, & Lin, 2013). Many times, these exercises don't involve the multiple steps—planning and process—involved in the writing process and they are not clearly connected to the unit's topic. They function as warmup activities or as useful transitional exercises between learning tasks, but we can't consider them a part of *writing instruction* that will build language and knowledge. Getting to advanced literacies for all means moving to the writing process as a crucial platform for fostering emerging and developing academic language and cementing content knowledge among ELs and their peers (Graham & Perin, 2007; Graham, Early, & Wilcox, 2014).

For writing to promote learners' language and cognitive skills, students need a structured, content-based approach to *all* writing assignments and tasks, for example, writing prompts, text questions, or narratives. Students need to have studied, in some depth, the material to be processed and written about. They also need supports and scaffolds to help them plan, discuss, and organize their ideas and develop an argument; incorporate and connect their words and sentences; and/or move from notes to a flowing paragraph. When students can accurately use new vocabulary and language structures in their writing, it has been shown that they can grasp the concept or the linguistic structure. Keep in mind that students, especially linguistically diverse learners, are often first exposed to academic language when they read written text, so once they start to use academic language in their own writing, we know that their language development is advancing.

What Does 21st-Century Writing Instruction Look Like?

Principal Lansdowne is participating in a team-level meeting with the eighth-grade team to develop a set of norms for responding to students' writing. Janie Walter has brought her students' most recent writing project: a short argumentative paragraph written in response to the question "Should the international community have imposed such harsh sanctions on Germany after World War I?" The goal of the assignment was to help students consolidate their thinking after reading several texts. Ms. Walter had students revise their short paragraphs after a brief text-based discussion. She asked students to imagine that this text was going to be read by a group of professors at the local college—and work with a peer to adjust their written language to match the audience. Kim Tran, another eighth-grade team member, notes that this revision routine, which students have used many times before in all of their classrooms, has supported Ms. Walter's students to use language more accurately and precisely ("mean" has been replaced with adjectives like "harsh" and "punitive").

INDICATORS OF HALLMARK 3 IN INSTRUCTION

Instructor communicates the importance of using target words when writing.	☑
Instructor acknowledges the challenges associated with learning new language and conveys an attitude that values experimenting with language by praising students' attempts at using target language when writing (i.e., an expectation that students will not likely use words correctly or precisely at first).	☑
Instructor builds-in writing routines/supports if these are not already an integral part of the curriculum.	☑
Instructor makes students aware of the classroom's writing routines, and students demonstrate comfort with these routines.	☑
Instructor uses writing as a method for consolidating thinking before and after reading (e.g., summarizing or responding by sharing his or her opinion).	☑
Instructor encourages students to use peers and texts as language resources when writing (e.g., to use language structures and words found in mentor texts or to adopt language that peers have used successfully in their own writing or speech).	☑
Instructor asks students to make use of previously taught words, language structures, and strategies for academic language learning when writing.	☑

Students have also added words that serve as signposts for readers—words like "however" and "as a result" that have been explicitly taught. Occasionally these are used incorrectly, but the eighth-grade teaching team interprets this to be a positive indication that a student is actively working to acquire this unfamiliar language. Tomorrow, Ms. Walter will have students return to the texts the class has read to find additional language and ideas to support their arguments. Using this additional information, they will add to this text because writing is an important part of every lesson.

Hallmark 4: Study a Small Set of High-Utility Vocabulary Words Needed to Master Language and Content

Because of the thousands of words our ELs and their peers need to learn to be academically successful, it's tempting to try to teach as many as possible—and very quickly! This "coverage" makes sense on its face, but it comes at a great cost: when we go for breadth over depth our students learn just a little about many words but not enough to use them independently in their speech or writing—and they don't learn *how* words work. This instructional time is not well spent. Vocabulary study represents a crosscutting strategy that can be used to build breadth and depth of topic knowledge (when studying content words like *photosynthesis* or *democracy*) or to acquire knowledge of general academic words that must be understood to regularly access text with success (words like *therefore* or *however*) (Graves et al., 2014). This general academic language is actually a significant source of reading comprehension difficulty for many ELs and their peers—even those from English-speaking homes (Uccelli et al., 2015).

At the same time, it is important to note that this is not really a "reading" problem—after all, many of our students read the words on the page accurately yet lack deep understanding of *what* they read (they are sometimes referred to as "word callers"; Valencia & Buly, 2004). To really support vocabulary learning, we should teach students specific words and concepts and *how* language and words work (instruction in word parts, like suffixes or prefixes, and Greek and Latin roots; Kieffer & Lesaux, 2007). Our general motto is that less is more! Research tells us that we should choose a small set of high-utility academic words (See, for instance, the Academic Word List: *www.victoria.ac.nz/lals/resources/academicwordlist*) that students will definitely need and then use those as a platform to teach word learning, to increase academic talk, and to promote more strategic reading. The deep language-learning process—one that supports advanced literacies—is vitally important and it takes time.

What Does 21st-Century Vocabulary Instruction Look Like?

As part of rounds, Principal Lansdowne and the other teachers in the fourth-grade team are visiting the classroom of fifth-grade teacher Maria Gonzalez. The goal is to observe her embedded vocabulary instruction so that the fourth-grade team can prepare their students for fifth grade. They've adopted a set of schoolwide protocols for teaching vocabulary, but Ms. Gonzalez is particularly comfortable with the routines and has invited her peers into her classroom. For this unit on photosynthesis, she is focusing on four target words that appear in the texts used throughout the unit: *solar, energy, result,* and *consequently.* Some of these words are specific to the topic (*solar, energy*) and others are general academic words (*result, consequently*). Ms. Gonzalez begins her lesson with a "draw for meaning" activity for the word *energy.* She asks students to draw an image that conjures up the idea of energy and then to write a sentence below using the word. Her students demonstrate different levels of knowledge of the word. Manuel, a student who had entered the school with little English in grade 4 wrote, "I have energies" below a picture he drew of children playing soccer. Tayja, on the other hand, had drawn a series of pictures and written a few sentences: "Both plants and animals need energy. Humans have energy from foods they eat, but plants get energy from sun." As the class engages in additional learning about the word *energy,* Ms. Gonzalez will have her students add to these initial definitions both to build their word knowledge and as a formative assessment of her teaching. Next, she engages the class in reading a short nonfiction text in which the target words appear. To provide her students with an opportunity to use the target words in speech, Ms. Gonzalez has students work in pairs. One student assumes the role of a biologist and the other the role of an interviewer, who is tasked with posing questions using the target words ("Can you explain how plants use solar energy?"). Finally, the

---

INDICATORS OF HALLMARK 4 IN INSTRUCTION

Instructor builds-in intentional exposures to target words and features if these are not already an integral part of the curriculum.	☑
Instructor uses the target words when speaking and writing with the class and encourages students to do the same.	☑
Writing is used as a method for practicing using the target words (e.g., before and after reading; end-of-unit projects; extended essays; structured summaries).	☑

SELECTING WORDS TO TEACH

For guidance on selecting words to teach and on delivering vocabulary and academic language instruction, refer to these resources:

Blachowicz, C., Ogle, D., Fisher, P., & Taffe, S. W. (2013). *Teaching academic vocabulary K–8: Effective practices across the curriculum.* New York: Guilford Press.

Townsend, D. (2015). Who's using the language?: Supporting middle school students with content area academic language. *Journal of Adolescent and Adult Literacy, 58*(5), 376–387.

Townsend, D., & Kiernan, D. (2015). Selecting academic vocabulary words worth learning. *The Reading Teacher, 69*(1), 113–118.

lesson concludes with each student writing a short summary of the reading in what Ms. Gonzalez calls "investigator logs."

After reminding students to use the target words, she explains that this short summary will be revised and extended as they read additional texts. She has selected these target words carefully and students will repeatedly encounter them across the 2-week unit. During the culminating project, students will create a museum exhibit explaining photosynthesis to younger children, which will require them to create a model or diagram that contains labels. Given their audience, students will again be called upon to define the target words. The fourth-grade teaching team is pleased to see that many of the activities they have adopted for teaching vocabulary are also present in fifth grade. Principal Lansdowne, in reflecting on the mission statement for advanced literacies instruction that her staff had drafted in the fall, which spells out some specific skills and competencies they are looking to build among all students, was delighted to note that students were using target academic vocabulary across reading, writing, and speaking tasks.

Hallmark 5: Use Schoolwide Protocols to Support Reading, Writing, Speaking, and Listening

This final hallmark revolves around the use of protocols. *Protocols* are tools that provide procedures and routines for reading, writing, speaking/listening, and problem solving in classrooms (McDonald, Mohr, Dichter, & McDonald, 2014). These protocols help students—and teachers—to engage in meaningful and efficient learning. In the schools we are in and out of, one of two scenarios emerge, both of which need revisiting if we are to get to advanced literacies for all: (1) no protocols are in widespread use; or (2) too many different protocols are taught—especially across classrooms and content areas—such that students don't have enough opportunity to gain mastery. By contrast, when a small number of protocols are taught and used consistently across the school site, protocols support different aspects of advanced literacies (e.g., learning unfamiliar vocabulary, comprehending text, discussing text, writing argumentative essays). They also make the mental processes engaged in by experienced readers, writers, and language users explicit to students who do not readily engage in this type of thinking on their own. In addition, many protocols—accountable talk (Michaels, O'Connor, Hall, & Resnick, 2002), reciprocal teaching (Palincsar & Brown, 1984), collaborative strategic reasoning (Vaughn et al., 2011), routines for teaching vocabulary (Lesaux, Kieffer, Kelley, & Harris, 2014), and process writing—are designed to support collaboration by providing a structure that makes partner and group work more productive. By helping students to co-construct knowledge, protocols help reduce the load placed on any one learner's working memory—or the ability to hold information in mind and manipulate it. Protocols also support the development of working memory skills—skills that help our students to manage and synthesize information from multiple sources or to keep track of the components of a multistep project (Janssen, Kirschner, Erkens, Kirschner, & Paas, 2010). By providing protocols and promoting collaborative work, we are scaffolding students' participation in advanced literacies tasks that would be too challenging for an individual learner working alone. While it may seem that creating predictable patterns can become tiresome to learners, our work with adolescents suggests just the opposite; predictability fosters a sense of competence and results in higher levels of motivation for many middle grade learners (Lesaux, Harris, & Sloane, 2012).

Therefore, getting to 21st-century literacies means stepping back and designing a coordinated, cohesive approach to building each student's advanced literacies—an approach that includes selecting a set of learning protocols. Our hope is for students to become so comfortable with protocols that they can deploy them with little effort, freeing up resources for students to focus on concept mastery.

What Does 21st-Century Instruction with Protocols Look Like?

After a productive day of working with her staff, Principal Lansdowne sits at her desk reflecting on what she has seen and heard in classrooms and team

INDICATORS OF HALLMARK 5 IN INSTRUCTION

Instructor builds-in intentional practice with schoolwide protocols.	☑
Instructor explains when, why, and how protocols are used to build students' skills to use protocols independently.	☑
Students show familiarity with protocols and are able to use them as a support for learning.	☑

meetings. In her mind, she keeps going back to the common practice of using specific learning routines and tasks across the classrooms—even though their content may differ widely. She reflected on Mr. Florence, who used the text-based question stems that the staff had selected together when interacting with his sixth graders, on Ms. Walters, who used the writing-revision routine employed by the eighth-grade team, and finally on Ms. Wong's fourth grade, where accountable language used in all classrooms permeated her students' discussions. Principal Lansdowne was heartened to see that the literacy team had spent its time so productively when it selected this common set of protocols during the previous summer institute. During the fall semester, teachers had invested instructional time establishing these routines, and now they are part of what we might call the *instructional fabric*.

Taking Action: Implementing Key Shift 1

Action Step 1: What Are Site-Specific Hallmarks?

Attempting to change the day-to-day texture of classroom instruction naturally involves a collaborative process between leaders and faculty as well as between and within grade-level teams. This is a multiyear process that begins with translating your Advanced Literacies Instruction Mission Statement into a set of schoolwide instructional practices and routines for implementation. This becomes your site-specific *Hallmarks of Advanced Literacies*. This chapter and the accompanying Leader's Tool 4.1 (in the Appendix) provide our articulation of what the hallmarks look like in action. Based on recommendations for fostering linguistically responsive classrooms and our own understandings of what comprises high-quality advanced literacies instruction, this checklist is designed to be comprehensive. Certainly, school sites can adopt the hallmarks as we present them in this chapter; or, based on a site's instructional context and student population, leaders may decide to expand on this core set of indicators. Ultimately, the goal should be to create a clear set of criteria for all faculty to assess their instruction and to set instructional goals.

Action Step 2: How Successful Is a Site's Implementation of the Hallmarks?

These site-specific hallmarks, when compiled into a checklist (see Leader's Tool 4.1 in the Appendix), can be used for observing teaching (peer, coaches, and administrators all benefit from using this tool) to gauge whether these high-level instructional practices and routines are part of everyday instruction and prove useful for setting instructional goals. This is not a tool for evaluating compliance; instead it should be used in the service of advancing instructional practice. Using a shared set of criteria for evaluating instruction and for setting professional goals has the consequence of creating a common vocabulary to discuss teaching and learning and does much to promote a cohesive and coherent learning experience for students.

Indicators of Successful Implementation

We began this chapter by highlighting the challenge inherent in promoting advanced literacies in an era in which we have just begun to understand what this instruction should look like. The hallmarks are designed to provide the

---

Short-Term Outcomes

- Site-based selection of a set of schoolwide instructional practices and routines for implementation (*Action Step 1*).

- Successful implementation of high-level instructional practices and routines across classrooms (*Action Step 2*).

Long-Term Outcomes

- Reduction in the number of students who need intervention.

- Reduction in the amount of money spent on interventions.

- Decreases in the numbers of students referred to special education.

FIGURE 4.3. Key Shift 1: Target outcomes.

necessary instructional road map. In schools that have successfully adopted this cohesive approach to advanced literacies instruction, leaders can anticipate the outcomes shown in Figure 4.3.

In the chapters that follow, we turn to the other shifts that are central to promoting advanced literacies at school sites. Specifically, we turn our attention to the second key shift in the next chapter by examining the role of data usage in a 21st-century literacy framework. We place this shift second, following this discussion of the instructional core. Why? Well, because if students have not had adequate high-quality opportunities to learn, we can't say with confidence that they are not responding to our instruction. However, this is exactly what we *are* saying when we look at assessment data and conclude that the majority of students require interventions without first assessing the strength of our daily instruction core (which leaders can do by using Leader's Tool 4.1). Instead, we should "begin assessing the instructional program prior to assessing the child" (Spinelli, 2008, p. 106). With this in mind, we turn next to examining the role of students' assessment data in 21st-century literacy.

CHAPTER 5

Placing Data at the Core
of the Literacy Improvement Effort

Principal Mary Lansdowne sighed as she put down the sheaf of papers she had been studying. The pile consisted of computer printouts and hand-written lists, a collection representing the scores of each student at Rosa Parks School on the latest wave of literacy testing. The school invested so much time in testing students, but the payoff of their labor was not always apparent in student performance. Mary was unsure of how the collective results yielded an overarching strategy for student improvement. In many cases the assessment data collected showed growth and even grade-level performance for individual students—students who would then come to be classified as "performing below grade level" on the fourth-grade state standards test. In other cases, it seemed like they had simply repeatedly documented which children were performing below grade level, but still lacked insight into which literacy skills needed bolstering. Principal Lansdowne was deeply troubled that so many of her students were struggling readers, but even more troubling was the thought that the assessments they had given simply didn't provide the information needed to craft a plan for improved teaching and learning from the earliest of years. Surely there had to be a way out of this?

As in many fields, effective educational practice starts with data. There's surely no thornier issue within today's educational system than that of assessment. Assessment, intended to be the cornerstone of instruction, has become a hot-button topic, in part because it has become misused, misunderstood, and overemphasized. One of the greatest missed opportunities in schools today has to do with how data are used in our improvement efforts. We have more data on our students than we have ever had—indeed, in many cases too much data to really make sense of. But in most schools we work with, we find that data are *not* actually central to overall literacy improvement efforts. And the questions we most commonly receive from the field—when we run institutes, hold trainings, and by e-mail—focus on assessment.

In fact, assessment is probably one of today's most prominent (and profitable!) educational enterprises—huge amounts of money, time, and energy are expended on administration, scoring, and reporting—at all levels of the system. Educational leaders, elected officials, community leaders, school leaders, teachers, parents, and students themselves are all deeply affected by an ongoing and often overwrought conversation about assessment and its results, yet few seem to truly understand it.

Indeed, it is puzzling, even disconcerting, that despite the precious resources spent, assessment remains one of the least understood enterprises in the education system. Often, conversations in media outlets, communities, and schools include inaccurate information about which assessments should be used for which purposes, and how the corresponding data can best be used to improve student learning. On the ground, this confusion has resulted in frustrations shared by leaders and educators alike across the nation. Unfortunately for our students, these misunderstandings have contributed to a growing belief among educators, parents, and the general public that assessment is a waste of time and money.

To be sure, a school population's test scores might drive a sense of urgency, even panic, about needed action. For example, we might hear instructional leaders and teachers enumerating percentages of learners who scored at low levels and in what areas on a state assessment. More commonly, assessment results are used to gain insight into a single struggling student and are central to case conferences, in large part due to compliance with policy. This is also the context in which we tend to be most comfortable with data, looking very closely at an individual's performance and profile. We might even group all of the students who performed at a certain level on a state end-of-year assessment for intervention. But these assessment activities are really activities on the edges—they are not central to the improvement effort and are not going to get us to advanced literacies for all.

We need assessments in our schools. No question about that. Without good data to inform instruction, our improvement efforts will always be limited. But we need assessment practices that use resources wisely and obtain appropriate information that propels our schools and students forward. And it

Problems to Be Addressed by Key Shift 2	Target Outcomes
• Inefficient, often frustrating or overwhelming, data analysis because data are in multiple places. • Time-consuming data analyses because of the primary focus on looking at each individual. • Faculty feel that programs, interventions and tireless efforts are "not working."	• Site-level discussions and planning on population trends and patterns of performance in data. • Reduction in the amount of time spent examining individuals' assessment results. • Reduction in literacy-related difficulties because instructional core has been tailored to reflect the needs of most students. • Rapid growth in the skills targeted by the intervention due to a closer match between the students' needs and the intervention.

FIGURE 5.1. Key Shift 2: Theory of change.

needn't be difficult or feel like a burden. In schools where data are central to the improvement effort, data become woven into the instructional fabric. See Figure 5.1 for a summary.

Organization of This Chapter

The topic of assessment might well be a book in and of itself and we do, indeed, refer the reader to particular titles,[1] including one that we have previously written that also features the Rosa Parks School squarely from the perspective of the assessments themselves and the process of linking data to instruction, from start to finish. Nevertheless, in this chapter, as part of this guide for educational leaders, we provide an "express" version of assessment, touching on three major issues and some corresponding suggested action steps that should be on the mind of each leader engaged in improvement efforts focused on advanced literacies for all. We have organized the chapter around these three distinct yet related issues, providing an overview of each (see Figure 5.2): (1) Too much time is spent administering assessments; (2) assessment data are not easily accessed for review and analysis; and (3) there are no clear links between data gathering and instructional outcomes.

---

[1]Boudett, City, and Murnane (2005); Lesaux and Marietta (2011); Stahl and McKenna (2012).

In addressing each of these three issues, we describe the architecture of a comprehensive assessment system that informs data-driven instruction to strengthen the site's efforts, assisting instructional leaders in choosing assessments to guide advanced literacies instruction, taking time and feasibility into account. We also attend to issues of implementation—the specific challenges and pitfalls related to assessment that are plaguing today's educational system and their solutions—and provide technical information about assessment types, to prevent issues of assessment data misuse. We close with a snapshot of assessment data use and related issues at Rosa Parks School in its literacy improvement efforts. At the end of this chapter, Appendix 5.1 addresses ques-

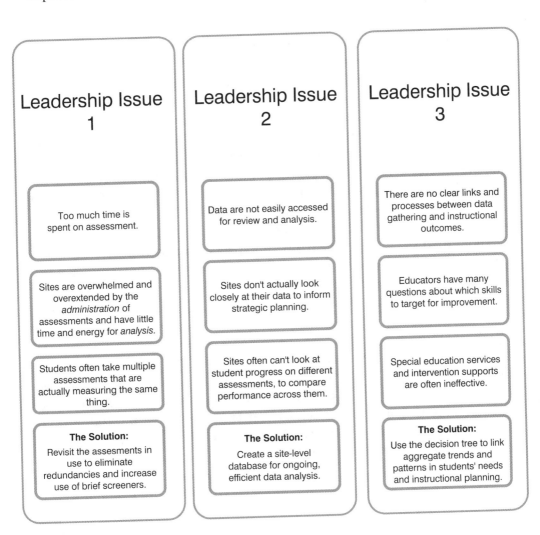

FIGURE 5.2. Key leadership issues.

tions regarding native language assessment and the assessment of newcomer students, who are still in the early stages of English language learning.

Issue 1: Too Much Time Is Spent on Assessment

One of our key goals for assessment is for the process to be supportive of instruction. This puts a premium on efficient action: we need to free up as much instructional time as possible if we hope to engage students in the integrated learning experiences that support reading and responding to complex texts. Not surprisingly, however, there is a general concern today that assessment has ballooned over the past decade—cutting into instructional time in epic proportions. And much of that assessment goes well beyond what's been mandated by the state as an annual outcome measure—there are the lengthy assessments administered one on one by a teacher to estimate reading level; there are shorter assessments that are increasingly administered on a computer, often used with struggling readers or that serve a test prep function; there are periodic district "benchmark" assessments designed to gauge student learning in light of the standards; and the list goes on.

Not long ago our team was part of an initiative involving a large urban district with high numbers of academically vulnerable students. It was revealed that this school district devoted no fewer than 90 hours of instructional class time, per year, on school-mandated literacy assessments. In some schools, over 200 hours of instructional time per year is spent administering (not scoring or interpreting) literacy assessments. This figure does not include the state test, which in this case began in third grade, or the assessments for math or other subject areas, or even curriculum-embedded assessments, such as informal oral assessments of reading comprehension or spelling tests.

We hear from teachers that the amount of time spent administering assessments can be so overwhelming that they feel they have little time left to consolidate the information and make instructional adjustments. Because the administration process is extended over several days or weeks, teachers often get results long after the school year is underway. In the end, it functions (and feels) like a compliance exercise rather than a systematic effort to improve student learning. This refrain is common among the many schools we have partnered with across the country to support their strategic planning efforts. So we worry a lot about the time and energy spent on administering assessments and the lack of resources available for analyzing the results and connecting them to instructional planning. We also worry a great deal about this experience for students, who are often taking multiple assessments that are *actually measuring the same thing.*

What is the key problem that underlies this scenario of so much time spent on individual assessment? In our experience the main problem lies in a mismatch between the types of assessments we're using—their intended purpose—and the information we're seeking and using them for. Each assessment type is better suited to certain purposes than others, and this careful match between purpose and use is not always well understood in school settings. We often see schools struggling to use assessment data productively because there is a lack of clarity on what information each assessment *can* provide. And very often the wrong types of assessment are used in light of the desired purpose, resulting in huge amounts of wasted time on the administration of the assessments. For this reason, we lay out here the three types of assessment tools that are part of a comprehensive literacy assessment battery—each serving a clear and specific purpose and each taking markedly different amounts of time to administer, as a function of the purpose. By including different types of measures in the assessment system, we gain an overall sense of our readers' performance and identify specific skills that may be placing individual learners at risk for reading difficulties. This level of information can be critical for the classroom, driving instruction in a way that will help students thrive as readers.

Understanding Different Assessment Types

In today's marketplace, there are three different types of assessment tools, each with a distinct purpose. As shown in Figure 5.3, the three assessment types are (1) formative, (2) screening, and (3) outcome.

There is *no hierarchy* to the three key types of assessment tools used to inform the design of advanced literacy instruction (formative, screening, and outcome); a comprehensive assessment system includes all three types. Yet, in our experience, schools are more likely to have some types of assessments than others—often formative and outcome, without any screeners in place.

Formative Assessments: Daily Nutrition and Exercise

Like the critical role that daily nutrition and exercise play in one's health, formative assessments sustain good teaching practices by informing instructional groupings and lesson planning, across the day and across school years. Whether asking questions to check for understanding, performing a running

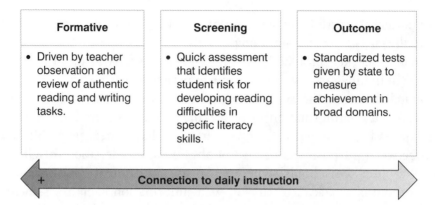

FIGURE 5.3. Assessment types.

record, or giving a unit or story test, teachers should, and are, regularly undertaking formative assessments. Some are part of a packaged literacy curriculum, such as a test or quiz students take after reading a book or chapter. Still other formative assessments emerge from a teacher asking questions and taking notes with the support of a rubric or observation checklist during a lesson.

Certain key features of formative assessments distinguish them from the two other categories of literacy assessment (i.e., screening and outcome):

1. These assessments as taking place largely "in meaningful, authentic contexts" as the behavior asked of a child during a formative assessment is very similar to what he or she might do on any given school day (if it is even separate from a lesson).
2. The results are immediately useful to the teacher in planning his or her approach to instruction.
3. They *do not* include an established or formal external benchmark against which to interpret student results. This is always the case, even

---

WHAT IS AN EXTERNAL BENCHMARK?

Calculated after testing a large sample of students representative of the population, external benchmarks provide a reference point to determine whether our students are performing "above," "below," or "at grade level." External benchmarks allow us to compare our students to students in the wider U.S. population—known as an external reference group.

when test publishers often set goals or guidelines for each grade level. While such instruments are marketed at times by publishers as tools for screening or tracking development compared to peers, they do not have the right protocols and procedures, nor have they been through the rigorous testing needed to ensure that they measure growth over time against an established and validated growth trajectory, to serve this purpose.

FORMATIVE ASSESSMENT PITFALL: PLANNING A FORMAL ASSESSMENT STRATEGY AROUND READING LEVELS

At first, it sounds extremely sensible to get a reading "level" for each student and then organize our instruction accordingly. And this goal may be helpful under certain circumstances, but not for identifying specific sources of difficulty or monitoring student progress in component literacy skills. There are a number of reasons for this failure to provide relevant information, many of which are not widely discussed in the field, but resonate with teachers and instructional leaders—many of whom have found themselves frustrated by the discrepancy between the time and energy spent on determining reading levels and students' growth as readers. Here, we discuss three key reasons that lead to this discrepancy between performance at a reading level and reading skills and competencies as established by external benchmarks:

1. Students are reading at their instructional level. To determine a child's reading level, we choose a text that we believe a student can read at his or her instructional level (i.e., with few miscues when reading the text aloud and with 80% accuracy as assessed by the teacher when asked simple postreading comprehension questions). These texts may not be on "grade level" for those students who are reading far below expected benchmarks and the testing format allows for teacher support. Therefore, very often, under these conditions, we overestimate student performance; anyone is a faster decoder and more fluent reader when engaging with simpler texts during an instructional event that is teacher-supported. Far too often, though, these are not the conditions that students are faced with when reading at grade level in the classroom or for assessment purposes.

2. We cannot identify the potential breakdowns students are experiencing when accessing complex, grade-level texts. For those readers who struggle, we cannot get an accurate sense of the scope or severity of difficulties in

ASSESSMENT TO UNCOVER THE FUNDAMENTALS

Imagine a professional basketball team has lost a game. In the end, the coach is given an analysis of performance that tells him that his players scored a very low percentage of 3-point shots. This information would likely be very valuable for informing practice and strategy going forward; after all, the coach knew that the fundamentals of their game were very sound. Contrast this, however, with Sky's role as an elementary girls' basketball coach. She had players who still had an emerging understanding of the fundamental rules of the game, some who were still working on basic shots, and some who needed more basic physical fitness and stamina to run down the court. In this case, practicing 3-point shots—a "nice to have" not "need to have" skill—would be a poor use of practice time. There would be key underlying issues to address; over time, as fitness, strength, and strategies were gained, players would begin to make 3-point shots. Assessment that only told Sky the players were doing poorly on 3-point shots and that prompted Sky to have them practicing those alone would be unlikely to produce important benefits or improve their game.

light of what is expected for that age and grade level when reading texts at a student's instructional level (like those used for formative assessment). Bear in mind, the complexity of sentences, number of rare and academic vocabulary words, and even the kind of topics introduced change rapidly from grade level to grade level; however, struggling readers in our classrooms may never be assessed using these texts (until they participate in an end-of-year state assessment) if we rely solely on formative measures. As a result, we have little indication of which features of grade-level texts are proving challenging to the students in a particular classroom and therefore we don't address these challenges instructionally. As we've discussed, many features of grade-level texts (e.g., academic language, sentence structures) pose specific challenges to linguistically diverse students, which means that addressing this oversight is especially pressing.

   3. *We cannot compare performance from student to student or aggregate the data to identify trends and patterns across children and classrooms.* In many schools, principals and reading coaches, along with other instructional leaders, are busy tallying up how many children are at which reading level in each grade. In fact, this practice is not a valid one (Christ, Monaghen, Zopluoglu, & Van Norman, 2013; Christ, Zopluoglu, Monaghen, & Van Norman, 2013). The conditions for determining a reading level mean that a level "J" for one student is not the same as a level "J" for another student. Why? Because when administering formative assessments we are gaining an understanding of how

a child performs when supported by his or her teacher; but from classroom to classroom how teachers support their students during assessment varies. For this reason, a "J" in one classroom might mean something different than a "J" in another. In fact, a recent study suggests that 16% of the variation in students' scores on curriculum-based measures of reading can be accounted for by differences in how educators administered and scored the assessment (Cummings, Biancarosa, Schaper, & Reed, 2014). As a result, reading-level assessments are not set up to draw these comparisons, nor can they inform the design of group instruction.

Screening Instruments: The Routine Check-Up

In the world of reading assessments, a screener is like an indicator of basic characteristics of health, such as blood pressure, temperature, height, and weight. These tools give us a clear indication of risk, either through set benchmarks or criteria, or by telling us how a child performs relative to peers of the same age or grade level (i.e., against "norms"). It is precisely this norming that allows screening assessments to identify the source of a problem and to signal the need for a corresponding treatment. What's crucial is that these tests often tell us about risks that may not be apparent from classroom interactions alone.

Just as the check-up uses specialized instruments (e.g., a blood pressure cuff), the actual tasks asked of a child during the screening assessment are different from day-to-day tasks completed as part of instruction. For example, the test may be timed, the child may be asked to read through passages that we know are above his or her reading level, or perhaps the child is asked to read a list of nonwords—a task that would never be part of classroom instruction. Unlike formative assessments, which are tied to instruction and performance in an authentic context, these are focused on tracking development in specific, separable literacy component skills.

Like the use of the thermometer at a doctor's visit, the screener result might signal a potential problem, such as a temperature that is well above 98.6°, but it is up to the doctor to dig further to uncover the underlying problem before prescribing a treatment. The same goes for reading rate—it is a quick indicator of whether this child's literacy skill development is "healthy." A performance below grade level signals the need to investigate the potential sources of this problem with fluency—and to design a plan of action. As with a routine doctor's visit, we use a range of indicators to examine literacy development in different component skills, such as fluency, vocabulary, and word-reading accuracy.

WHY FORMATIVE ASSESSMENTS CAN'T FUNCTION AS SCREENERS

Many of today's schools do not have screeners in place—but they are using individualized, formative assessments for this purpose, using up huge amounts of time to individually assess each and every child two to three times per year using a very comprehensive, in-depth protocol to arrive at a reading level. This is not only inefficient but these practices do not line up with the purpose of formative assessments. They were not designed as screening tools that provide data that can and should be aggregated across students and classrooms. Formative assessments, by design, are not standardized in nature—one teacher's running record or miscue analysis is not the same as another's and in many cases students' levels fluctuate from day to day and text to text, and we are never sure of exactly the source of challenge or breakdown. What we want to do with all students is screen them for potential risk on specific skills and competencies using brief, standardized measures—we quickly need a "green light," "yellow light," or "red light" for each reader in each specific skill or competency assessed. Then, we have time for more in-depth assessment to design tailored instruction to support those who may be struggling.

SCREENING ASSESSMENT PITFALL: THERE ARE NO SCREENERS IN PLACE

Many of today's schools do not have screeners in place. Per the discussion above, what we want to do with all students is to screen them for potential risk on component skills using brief, standardized measures—we quickly need a "green light," "yellow light," or "red light" for each reader in each specific skill or competency assessed. Then we have time for more in-depth assessment to design tailored instruction to support those who may be struggling. Instead, as discussed above, many schools are using *individualized formative assessments* for this purpose, using up *huge* amounts of time to individually assess each and every child two to three times per year using a very comprehensive, in-depth protocol to arrive at a reading level. This is not only inefficient, but these practices do not line up with the purpose of formative assessments. They were not designed as screening tools that provide data that can and should be aggregated across students and classrooms. Recall that formative assessments, by design, are not standardized: one teacher's running record or miscue analysis is not the same as another's and in many cases students' levels fluctuate from day to day and text to text, and we are never sure of the exact source of challenge or breakdown.

Outcome Assessments: Stepping on the Scale

Outcome assessments are those formal assessments typically given once or twice annually, often group-administered to all students in a grade level or school. In today's climate of assessment-based accountability, outcome assessments in schools are usually standards-based tests that are mandated and standardized. The main purpose of outcome assessments it to provide an indication of *the overall achievement levels* of the test taker in a given domain. Just as physicians use a patient's weight to place him in bands (e.g., normal weight, overweight), outcome test results are often used to categorize students (and, in turn, schools) as "warning," "in need of improvement," "proficient," or "advanced" in broad academic areas. They are the "farthest" from daily instruction, but they are also the results that are often the most informative for school, district, and state leaders who are focused on improvement, literacy rates, and tracking the results of reform efforts. The results on outcome measures can tell us about the extent to which a school's reading program is meeting students' needs, or if certain groups (ELs, African American students, students with an identified learning disability) appear to be responding better than others.

OUTCOME ASSESSMENT PITFALL: ATTEMPTING TO TEACH BASED ON ITEM ANALYSIS

As previously mentioned, in the last 10 years we have noticed a growing trend to measure and then to teach the specific *performances* associated with expert reading comprehension that are often evaluated on our outcomes assessments. This trend is evident in the language of many state's standards and in the items that comprise standardized achievement tests (e.g., Stanford) or the rather recent, emerging line of "test prep" assessments (e.g., Achieve 3000). There is a tendency to examine the results of outcome assessments at the item level— to figure out the types of items groups of students struggled with and then go back and teach to support this understanding. Perhaps the most universal example is "finding the main idea" in a passage. An ever-growing industry of assessments aim to capture whether a student can identify the main idea of a passage—usually through multiple-choice items presented after the child reads a passage. You might be scratching your head, wondering what is wrong with this practice. After all, don't we want students to be able to determine the main idea of a grade-level passage?

As described in Chapter 2, the problem is that finding the main idea— among many other similar performances or exercises—is just that—a reading *performance.* It is not a specific skill. That is, to perform the task at hand, in this case to find the main idea, the reader draws on *many* component skills and composite competencies and initiates those in concert with one another. In turn, when a student is not able to find the main idea, we still do not know why. Did the student struggle because he or she could not decode unfamiliar words? Or because he or she read too slowly? Or was it that the vocabulary was too advanced? Perhaps the topic was unfamiliar, and he or she did not have enough background knowledge? Or might it even be that he or she was completely unfamiliar with the tone, the genre, or the whole enterprise of reading an isolated passage and filling in bubbles? There is, of course, a chance that all of the other pieces are in place, and the student simply needs more instruction and practice in finding the main idea—generating the gist amid the details. We do not know. And when we do not know, we are less likely to teach the specific skills and competencies that make up these literacy performances and underlie outcomes—and therefore meet our readers' needs. Instead, we are likely to teach the literacy performance (teaching the main idea), not teach the skills that underlie this literacy performance.

TEST PREP ASSESSMENT PITFALL: TAILING A MOVING TARGET

What we call "test prep" assessments are a new and growing portion of the assessment marketplace. These are assessments that use a previously administered (and now publicly released) version of a state test to generate similar items and scores. The idea behind test prep assessment is to mimic an old test with the goal of predicting performance on the next state assessment. There are many problems with this approach.

First, state assessments change from year to year. Granted, sometimes these changes only reflect subtle shifts in the content; but other years there are major changes in content and format. Second, these tests do not provide information on breakdowns in particular literacy skills. Remember, if a student cannot find a main idea, we do not know why this is the case from the data provided by these assessments.

For these reasons, test prep assessments sit outside of an assessment system that informs literacy instruction. They might be thoughtfully and sparingly used as a preparation aid for a state test—with the same attention and weight given to them as to any other test prep activity. What they absolutely should not do is inform an approach to literacy instruction.

Taking Action: Implementing Key Shift 2

Action Step 1: Conduct an Assessment Inventory (for Strategic Planning)

In our work with schools, the first thing we often do when tackling the issue of assessment is start with supporting teams of administrators and teachers to conduct an assessment inventory with the goal of accomplishing three things:

1. To match each assessment type to its current purpose in the system.
2. To ensure there is no redundancy with respect to skills measured within the system.
3. To log time spent on assessment, in numbers of hours per year.

What we have observed in countless meetings is that most schools included formative assessment and outcome assessment, but very few had screening assessments in place. When teams carry out their inventory, we find that at least 90% of the time formative measures are being used as screening instruments, not only violating the technical properties and purpose of these formative measures, but also the principle that screening is, by design, supposed to be very brief in nature.

The second dimension of the inventory work typically reveals that, even as there is a problem between assessment type and function within the battery, there are often redundancies within the battery itself. For example, many schools have several measures of literacy performances, including multiple assessments that ask children to identify the main idea of a passage. Another common example of redundancy includes multiple measures of how accurately a child can read graded passages, thus identifying the child's reading "level." At still other sites, there may be many assessments of how quickly and accurately students can decode words.

If we hold to the notion that each screening assessment should be administered on a schedule to gain a snapshot or estimate of a reader's ability in a particular skill or competency, that is, to get the green, yellow, or red light, then there is no room for redundancy—any and all redundancy must be eliminated. This is also true across assessment types in the battery; there is no value-add to having two measures that provide reading levels, two measures that estimate reading achievement, or even two measures of comprehension of grade-level texts. For more detail, nuance, and any follow-up information needed for instructional purposes, whether tomorrow's lesson or next week's instructional groupings, we turn to the formative assessments that are in the teacher's toolkit. They are administered on his or her time, as needed, and guided by his or her knowledge of where the breakdown may be occurring.

Finally, it's often the case that teams have actually never sat down and calculated just how much time is used for assessments required at the site. While the first thing that comes to mind for teams are the number of days allocated for the state-level testing, the vast majority of time, in fact, is generally spent on assessments that were chosen at the district level or school level. In most cases, we are not aware that formative assessments mandated by a principal can easily take up 90 hours of instructional time per year, particularly if they are correctly administered.

What we suggest here is to complete an inventory to first identify the types of assessments in place, and then consider what each assessment measures and how much time each takes to administer.

Inventory of Assessment Types

Equipped with the information from this chapter, you should now be ready to generate an inventory of your current assessments, using Leader's Tool 5.1 in the Appendix. The goal here is not to be exhaustive: there is no need to write down every spelling test or unit test given to students. Instead, the focus is on assessments that are part of a formal battery and required (or mandated) by the state, district, or school. In this process, you will write down one assessment on each line, and then determine the assessment *type*. You can use the check boxes to mark whether the assessment is formative, screening, or outcome. Take any important notes on how the determination was made. What did you notice when you filled out the assessment inventory? Perhaps your school primarily relies on formative assessments to understand students' literacy performance and growth—a common practice in schools around the United States.

Inventory of Time Budgeted for Schoolwide Assessment

How much time is spent on assessment across the school? To arrive at this number, use Leader's Tool 5.1. Discuss the total time spent on administration with your colleagues. For individually administered assessments, you will need to determine the amount of time spent administering the test to one child, then multiply it by the number of students in a class. If an assessment is given multiple times per year, you also need to multiply by the number of administration periods. For example, if a test takes 45 minutes to administer for each child, and is given three times per year, multiply 45 times the number of students in the class times 3. This will give an estimate of the amount of time it takes for one class at that grade level. If there are slight differences between two classrooms at the same grade level, based primarily on differences in the number of students, write down the middle number of hours. As a group, record how many hours are spent for each grade to create a schoolwide record.

Action Step 2: Plan a Comprehensive Yet Streamlined Assessment System for Your Site

After studying the site's inventory, the literacy team may look to revise its approach to assessment. Among others, one key decision at sites we've worked with is to include screeners, to address the time-consuming and problematic practice of using their formative measures as screening tools. As a first step in creating this comprehensive yet streamlined assessment system, the team typically decides to administer screening assessments on a set schedule three times per year (see Figure 5.4). By attending to the typical developmental progression for each skill, they then determine a timetable for assessment that accurately reflects grade-level expectations for literacy development. They also appropriately decide that because formative assessments are closely tied to daily instruction, teachers should determine their timing and administration (Figure 5.4).

This strategy often represents a major shift—previously, teachers would have been required to administer formative assessments, such as Fountas and Pinnell's Benchmark Assessment or the DRA, on a set calendar. They would also be compelled to report scores to the principal or data coordinator. We recommend abandoning this practice because there is no other use for data from these assessments beyond designing tomorrow's lesson or a targeted support plan for an individual student. For that reason, they should only be administered as needed. And in making this change, there is a huge savings in collective time and energy. In fact, one of the greatest benefits of implementing

> **A VERY IMPORTANT REMINDER: IT IS BETTER TO REDUCE THE TOTAL NUMBER OF ASSESSMENTS THAN TO SIMPLY ADD ON MORE SCREENING MEASURES.**
>
> When we simply expand the assessment battery, we are increasing the burden placed on students and teachers. In contrast, a vertically aligned, schoolwide system that ensures timely screening and attention to the development of specific skills and competencies is brief, efficient, and conducive to freeing up time for looking at data.

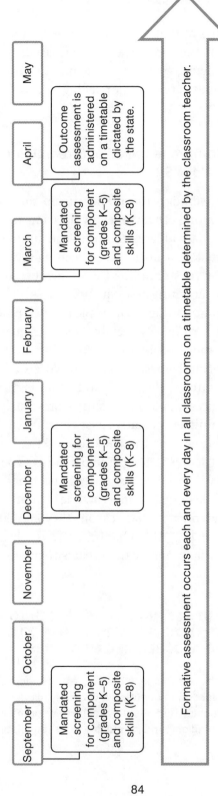

FIGURE 5.4. Action Step 2: Plan a comprehensive yet streamlined assessment system for your site.

screeners is that they can *reduce* the amount of time spent on assessment. We have found that two different screeners, for example, at three points in the year, can be administered in no more than 26 hours, approximately half the amount of time used for assessment in many schools today.

Issue 2: Data Are Not Easily Accessed for Review and Analysis

As we think about implementing an assessment system, we start by noting the characteristics that comprise an efficient and effective data system. The most actionable of these is the creation of a data system that makes scores clear and accessible for translating into practice (Shapiro, Zigmond, Wallace, & Marston, 2011). As soon as all test administration is complete, it is important to have one common system where results can be aggregated. Without this shared system in place, it is challenging to understand student performance from year to year or to foster a common language around assessment for faculty. We recommend creating a database where scores from all assessments can be compiled side by side, making it easy to see relative areas of strength and weakness for individuals, classrooms, grade levels, even the school population at large. Today, several assessments come packaged with advanced software options, including databases that generate detailed score reports. While this software offers advantages, we need to take note that not all software systems across assessments can be linked. School leaders and teachers are then left with disparate data, and must look back and forth between databases in order to understand the overall instructional profile of their students.

Action Step 3: Create a Data System That Makes Scores Clear and Accessible for Translating into Practice

The most straightforward system—and the most economical—is a simple electronic spreadsheet stored on a secure, shared drive, with a separate "sheet" for every classroom or grade level. Workbooks can be formatted so that cells are automatically color-coded based on the value of the scores that are entered. It's a matter of setting threshold numbers for "high risk," "some risk," and "low risk" scores, such that cell values within these ranges will automatically turn red, yellow, and green, respectively. Once the table is formatted, a small team of school staff can enter results into this shared workbook, which automatically generates a color-coded table (as well as figures) where students' instructional needs are highlighted and visible across the school (see Figure 5.5).

Ms. Jackson's First-Grade Class				
Name	Letter Identification	Phonics	Receptive Vocabulary	Listening Comprehension
Ana	Some Risk	High Risk	High Risk	High Risk
Bailey	Low Risk	High Risk	High Risk	High Risk
Curtis	Low Risk	High Risk	High Risk	High Risk
Devonte	Low Risk	Low Risk	Some Risk	Low Risk
Elian	Low Risk	Low Risk	High Risk	Some Risk
Kim	Low Risk	Low Risk	Low Risk	Low Risk
Georgia	Some Risk	Low Risk	High Risk	Some Risk
Harold	Low Risk	Some Risk	Low Risk	High Risk
Isaac	Low Risk	Low Risk	High Risk	Low Risk
Josiah	Low Risk	Low Risk	Low Risk	Low Risk
Kimberlee	Some Risk	High Risk	Low Risk	Some Risk
Leander	Low Risk	Low Risk	Low Risk	Low Risk
Monique	Low Risk	Low Risk	Some Risk	High Risk
N'Shawn	Low Risk	Low Risk	Some Risk	High Risk
Oliver	Low Risk	Low Risk	Some Risk	High Risk
Chris	High Risk	High Risk	High Risk	High Risk
Patrick	Low Risk	Low Risk	Some Risk	High Risk
Renee	Low Risk	Low Risk	Some Risk	High Risk

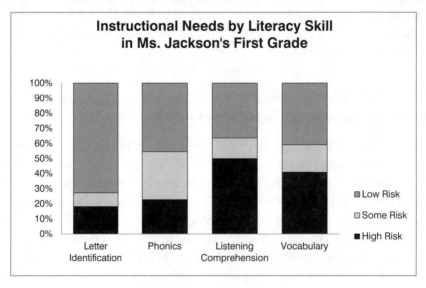

FIGURE 5.5. Classroom-level data.

The next year, students' scores can be cut and pasted into their new classrooms, providing an easy-to-access archive of their literacy development. In addition, spreadsheets and workbooks can easily generate various tables and charts, as well as "sort" students from lowest to highest scores. In a school climate that is sensitive to others viewing scores, it is possible to set up a password-protected workbook for each teacher on a shared drive that is still viewable by school leaders.

As part of the testing calendar, dates for scoring and reporting are essential. To support teachers in understanding their classroom-level data, we've seen value in setting up data teams, which use the database to efficiently produce an organized and straightforward table of student scores and a graph summarizing their key areas of strength and weakness. Often, these data teams are individuals in the school with some expertise in literacy and second language development, who can support classroom educators in making sense of test results. The use of collaborative teaming isn't trivial; when teachers work in these structures, they often make fewer referrals to special education, especially for linguistically diverse students (Gravois & Rosenfield, 2006).

We have also found it useful for teachers to meet in grade-level teams—or "problem-solving" teams—to share and discuss their findings (Klingner & Eppolito, 2014). Very often the areas of greatest need are shared across classrooms, opening up dialogue on how best to support these learners given their age and the curricular materials available (Haager, Klingner, & Aceves, 2009). In these initial meetings, the color- (or symbol-) coded tables and charts help focus participants on the task at hand: to talk about instructional needs at a classroom level. These teams shouldn't just meet to examine screening data; they should also look at formative assessment data to understand individual learners' development across the academic year.

Issue 3: There Are No Clear Links and Processes between Data Gathering and Instructional Outcomes

Once data have been gathered and organized, we face the daunting task of linking them to instruction. Here, we attempt to answer a question that we have often been asked: *What would a model linking data to instruction, which will result in advanced literacy, look like?* To begin to answer this question we provide an organizing structure—a decision tree—for understanding and undertaking the process of building an instructional core that fosters advanced literacy skills by focusing on the aggregate needs of a school population surfaced in the data *and* for identifying students whose needs are not otherwise being met by the core curriculum and who will require targeted instruction. The decision tree brings clarity by providing a set of organizing steps and their corresponding questions for school-based teams to follow; it is a flexible framework, one that can be applied at the level of the school and the classroom.

The Decision Tree Organizing Structure: An Overview

In Figure 5.6, you will see that the decision tree starts out with a key question about an individual student who is struggling: *Is the student's problem unusual given peers' performance?* Before generating a plan for any struggling student, we have to be able to answer this key question. You may be asking, *How would we know if a student's difficulties are different?* To answer this question we must have an assessment system in place as early as PreK, and its implementation must be ongoing, sustained, and timely throughout the school years if the data

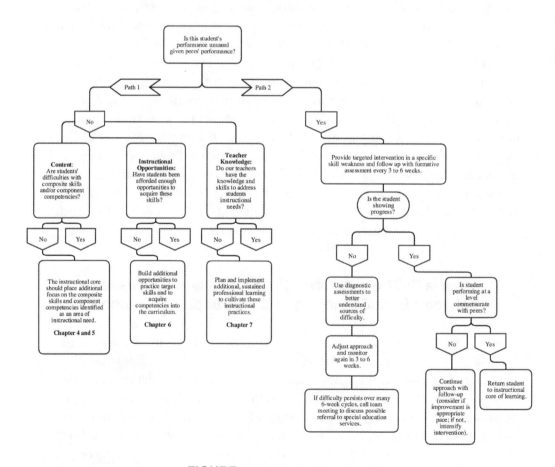

FIGURE 5.6. The decision tree.

they provide are to drive instructional change. The data must also be orga-nized to identify population trends and to highlight individual students with needs unlike their peers (see Issue 2).

You may recall the notion of a "true peer" introduced in Chapter 3. When attempting to determine if a linguistically diverse student is performing differ-ently (either in rate or level of learning) than same-grade counterparts, we will need to hold this reader up against true peers: students with similar language proficiency levels and who are currently experiencing similar opportunities to acquire English in the classroom (Brown & Doolittle, 2008). In sum, the ques-tion we are asking when examining the data for ELs or nonmainstream dialect speakers is this: *Is the student's problem unusual given peers' performance?*

Once we're able to answer that question (*Is the student's problem unusual given peers' performance?*), it takes us down one of two pathways: the first focuses on adjusting the instructional core before locating the problem at the level of the individual (Path 1) while the second focuses on designing literacy interventions to support individual strugglers (Path 2). In other words, Path 1 focuses our attention on a learner's need *in relation* to his or her classmates, while Path 2 keeps us focused on the individual. In walking these two path-ways, we address the need to focus on the instructional core in settings where high numbers of students are considered at risk for reading difficulty. These data often tell a disheartening story: that linguistically diverse students' needs are not being met. The tendency has been to look for supplemental interven-tions, but to move instructional practice forward and support all students to develop advanced literacy skills, schools need to be able to respond to this data differently—by tailoring the instructional core and by providing intervention only to those readers who persistently struggle despite maximal opportunities to learn and practice their skills and competencies through daily instruction.

Walking Path 1: Strengthening the Instructional Core by Placing Data at the Center

You may wonder why we place such a heavy focus on understanding a learner's profile in relation to peers, especially in settings where high numbers of stu-dents are linguistically diverse or are considered at risk for reading difficulty. In our extensive work with schools, we have all too often observed the negative consequences that occur when a student's data are not situated in the broader context of the student population. That is, viewed separately from his peers, a linguistically diverse student may appear to be a struggling reader. Viewed in relation to his peers, he may demonstrate similar strengths and challenges as the *majority* of his EL and English-only classmates—and even have difficulties that are not as severe as some. After all, the students filling our classrooms and schools are many times from the same neighborhoods and share a common linguistic history or set of environmental risk factors—for example, many are growing up in homes impacted by poverty (Bhattacharya, 2010). At the level of the student population, this shared background shapes students' needs, resulting in some collective strengths and weaknesses.

This is not to say that we wouldn't support this student's literacy development—we absolutely would, but within the instructional core. We would not refer this learner for literacy intervention services just yet because we certainly can't refer the majority of students nor can we claim with certainty that this student population has had sufficient, tailored opportunities to learn the skill or competency (i.e., until we have taken a thorough inventory to determine whether high-quality opportunities to learn are present in the classroom environment; see Leader's Tools 4.1 and 6.1 in the Appendix). In other words, the trends in the data suggest that the best support is likely at the level of the instructional core (i.e., the daily plan for learning and teaching) so that his or her needs and those of his or her classmates are better met and our instructional time and learning opportunities are maximized. The instructional core is, after all, our most significant instructional resource. Keep in mind that students spend nearly 30 hours each week in the classroom, nearly 1,080 hours per year.

When identifying ways to build a stronger instructional core, we look to examine not only the content and skills taught (Chapters 4 and 6); we must also consider the teacher's skill and knowledge in delivering and adapting the instruction for linguistically diverse students (Chapter 7) and the nature of the instructional opportunities provided (Chapters 4 and 6) (Elmore, 2008). Armed with insights into population trends and patterns, conventional wisdom would suggest that meeting the particular needs of our population entails looking at each element in turn and systematically planning to tailor each.

Curriculum Content and Skill Building: Linking What Is Measured to What Is Taught

To answer the call of the standards to teach advanced literacy skills, schools and districts have adopted both curriculum and instructional strategies that are designed to positively impact student achievement. Given what we know about advanced literacies, these programs should build knowledge and literacy skills. Curricula, however, often place a lopsided focus on one or the other. For instance, a curriculum may concentrate on building literacy skills—by teaching phonics systematically and by teaching what we refer to as cognitive reading strategies, for example, the skills to make inferences, to summarize a text, and to reread when you recognize that you've not understood the text. Rarely do these curricula *also* include enough rich texts and opportunities for text-based discussion and extended writing. Sometimes the weaknesses we observe at a population level can be linked to these curricular gaps; students have not developed the skills because we've not taught them. In this instance, we must build out from an existing core to ensure that we have adequate skill coverage, using trends in the data for guidance. In particular, curriculum often needs to be adapted for ELs (see e.g., Francis et al., 2006; Gersten & Baker, 2000; and Samway & McKeon, 2007, for additional guidance on "best practices" with ELs). In Chapter 6, we offer additional insight into selecting and adapting curricula to meet these goals.

Teachers' Professional Skills and Knowledge

Learning to teach in this new era of advanced literacies instruction requires professional development that builds these new competencies. Identifying what professional development is needed begins by understanding the trends and patterns of student performance in our schools. While multiple formats are used for professional learning, the important element is not where or how the professional learning takes place, but that it is targeted to the key areas of instructional need identified through the assessment process; it is crucial that educators approach professional learning with a clear goal for their own work (for additional guidance, see Chapter 7; Villegas-Reimers, 2003).

Professional learning also helps educators to make the leap from scores to effective lessons; indeed, there is clear documentation of data-driven instruction gone awry when we attempt to "teach to the test" (e.g., Goodman, 2006, presents a collection of examples around misuses of the DIBELS). Let's turn briefly to examine a composite competency that we recommend be assessed as part of a screening battery and which underpins advanced literacies: reading comprehension. Rather than thinking of reading comprehension as an isolated "skill," we can think of it as a proxy for some important component skills, including vocabulary, background knowledge, and even familiarity with stories and other texts. In this case, simply having a student answer multiple-choice reading-comprehension questions like the ones that appear on a screener, without building up these component skills, will do little to move the needle on his or her reading comprehension. What is needed where many students struggle with reading comprehension—a common pattern in linguistically diverse settings—is instruction that targets this wider array of skills. Helping teachers to draw conclusions about instructional priorities based on data is often a useful focus of professional development and linked with improvement in the instructional core.

Instructional Opportunities

It is important to remember that even a solid curriculum delivered by a skilled teacher will falter if students haven't been given the chance to develop mastery. Often, the patterns of strength and challenge surfaced in assessment are simply indicators of instructional opportunity. After all, knowing how to proficiently engage in any literacy task (or any task at all!) is the result of practice; but, as we attempt to teach a greater number of skills and more content across the instructional day, opportunities for students to make use of their newly acquired skills are often few and far between. This notion of instructional opportunities is particularly salient for ELs who are acquiring knowledge of language and content simultaneously. While these students may be afforded multiple exposures to content or skills, they may still struggle because English—the medium through which the instruction is delivered—is unfamiliar. In classrooms teaching larger numbers of ELs, opportunities to make use of developing English language skills and knowledge should be frequent. But this also means making choices about what not to teach; there is only so much time in the instructional day.

The simple act of charting instructional time can help leaders identify how their literacy block fits with student needs. While it is important to continue to provide balanced instruction, you may find that more time could be "budgeted" toward certain key skills areas. In order to gain a strong understanding of how instructional time is being invested, a colleague, mentor, or instructional leader can observe teaching and chart the time spent on instruction: how many minutes are devoted to phonics, discussion questions, writing, and so on. This is the beginning of a productive discussion centered on a few key questions: How do these activities relate to the identified area of need? What small adjustments hold the potential for big differences? Where can instruction be intensified?

Path 1 in Action

In one meeting, Principal Lansdowne and members of the data team (a reading specialist, a teacher from each grade, and an ESL specialist) began by examining the data from each grade level to identify patterns. The team was immediately struck by the vast number of children identified in red ("warning") in grades 4 and 5. Over 50% of the students appeared to need additional support to meet grade-level expectations. A small number of students appeared to be struggling in ways that differed from their peers. For instance, three children in grade 5 were struggling with word-reading skills, although the majority were not. What most fifth graders did have in common, however, was very low scores on a vocabulary measure and low scores on an assessment of reading comprehension. The team was particularly distressed to find that so many ELs appeared to be struggling with these skills—many of these students had been with them since kindergarten, had ESL services, and appeared to have come such a long way. But clearly they hadn't come far enough, and middle school was fast approaching. They also noted how many students with these under-developed comprehension skills were *not* ELs.

Given that time, resources, and teachers were always in short supply, pro-viding supplementary interventions to nearly 30 students in each grade was neither feasible nor efficient—too many children demonstrated this similar pattern to respond case by case. This cued the team to think about ways to strengthen the core of instruction—instruction provided to all students—with respect to language-learning opportunities. In subsequent meetings with the grade-level teams, the group will discuss how the core curriculum could be adjusted to better meet learners' needs. Specifically, children in grades 4 and 5 will require many more opportunities to acquire text-comprehension skills and to interact with rich texts, which may lead to shifts in how instructional time is allocated through the day. They will also discuss how the teachers in these grades could be better supported through professional development and new instructional resources. Of course, those children with difficulties unlike their peers will receive additional support (e.g., three fifth graders who dem-onstrated word-reading difficulties may need intensive phonics); most chil-dren, though, are not candidates for targeted, individualized intervention, but instead represent the need for a targeted effort at the classroom and school levels. Why? Because difficulties appear to be a weakness in the instructional core and what they need is enriched daily instruction.

Who Is Involved in Strengthening the Instructional Core?

When planning to strengthen the instructional core to improve daily learning and teaching for all, many stakeholders should be involved. In the case of the Rosa Parks School, the team was composed of reading specialists, classroom teachers, and ESL specialists; each individual brought unique knowledge to the table. This led to richer discussions about what the curriculum and their instruction did well and helped the team to identify ways that both could be strengthened for the many ELs and their peers with similar needs in grades

4 and 5. For instance, the curriculum used in grades K–5 had a very strong sequence for building word-reading skills, and by fourth grade the vast majority of students demonstrated grade-level mastery. In contrast, the team noted weaknesses in their curricular plans and materials; the basal readers provided by the curriculum and used as the central texts were not very conceptually rich. Because most students were not reading on grade level and had little opportunity to read grade-level texts, they were missing out on the exposure to ideas and vocabulary provided by these texts. While this curriculum may have worked well in a population where few children were reading below grade level, the population at Rosa Parks did not fit this profile. In hindsight, Principal Lansdowne and her team were not surprised that students had struggled when presented with the screening assessments.

This suggested to the team that they would need to better support teachers to provide instruction that went beyond a focus on the curricular texts and involved more experiences with language and ideas. These changes would not just be needed in the upper grades, where reading difficulties manifested themselves, they would be needed urgently at the lower grade levels, beginning with kindergarten. Beyond English language arts, the team saw opportunities for this work to continue in other content areas. This would involve a collaborative effort to "build out" from the existing core. In the subsequent chapters in this book, we discuss in greater depth how to identify weaknesses and engage in the work of enriching your core curriculum (Chapter 6). We build off of a core curriculum because it provides a schoolwide platform for teaching reading skills and a shared starting point for instructional discussion and professional development. It also brings consistency to the day for students, across the years.

Walking Path 2: Maximizing Opportunities to Learn for Students Who Struggle Persistently

The second pathway of the decision tree identifies readers whose literacy needs are unlike those of their peers in either type (e.g., students who persistently struggle with word-reading skills) or severity. Notably, a single data point collected via screening initiates targeted instructional support, but is never used to make high-stakes decisions about a student (e.g., to determine special education classification).

Because language development can sometimes "look like" a learning difference, schools should keep these considerations in mind when examining linguistically diverse students' literacy data and when referring students to interventions:

- ELs often have receptive vocabularies that are larger than their productive (or expressive) vocabularies; this is also true for many native English speakers and nonmainstream dialect speakers. *It is not an indication of a learning difficulty.*
- Errors in speech (e.g., syntax, word order) are common for linguistically diverse students and are signs that the student is making progress; *these are not indicators of a learning difficulty* (de Jong & Harper, 2004). For non-mainstream dialect speakers the use of particular grammatical structures common in AAE (i.e., the use of the habitual *be* as in "We be eating"), but not in mainstream English dialects, actually signals that the student *is* acquiring knowledge of language structures that he or she has heard.
- Language acquisition is an uneven process and some skills may develop more quickly than others. Students may demonstrate grade-level vocabulary knowledge, but still struggle with grammar.
- Students acquiring academic English as an additional dialect may not recognize when this language is expected to be used to complete a literacy task. Educators should make these expectations transparent.
- Linguistically diverse students who demonstrate persistent difficulties with spelling, awareness of sound–letter correspondence, poor memory, or lack of knowledge of the alphabetic principle after receiving adequate instruction *may be experiencing a learning difficulty* (Nelson et al., 2003; Al Otaiba & Fuchs, 2002).

Students who demonstrate issues like those in the last bullet point above are often our best candidates for literacy interventions.[2] This is because these types of literacy difficulties are the most amenable to targeted, intensive interventions (see Figure 5.6)

Once we've decided to provide a student with intervention, many factors can undermine effective implementation (see Figure 5.7). In particular, an issue worth calling out is the lack of collaboration that often occurs around intervention planning. School-based teams need to organize in order to coordinate scheduling, establish groupings, and arrange for continued progress monitoring. These efforts ensure that students will receive an additional "double dose" of the instruction that has been provided as part of the core.

---

[2]For additional information on interventions, see Daly, Neugebauer, Chafouleas, and Skinner (2015).

Low-quality interventions	• Not scientific, research-based, or shown to be effective with linguistically diverse populations.
Insufficient implementation process	• Frequency and duration of the intervention is insufficient. • Fidelity of implementation is not monitored. • Knowledge of educators about the program/initiative is underdeveloped.
Inconsistent professional development	• Staff transition in/out of schools, training opportunities are rare.

FIGURE 5.7. Factors that undermine effective implementation.

Path 2 in Action

When Principal Lansdowne and her team looked at the data, 15–20% of students in grades K–3 had either (1) difficulty with skills that most others had mastered; or (2) a similar profile as their peers, but showed much more severe difficulties. This suggested to Janet and her team that the core curriculum and its implementation was generally meeting the students' needs. When the data team does meet to discuss the results of the assessments with the teachers at each of these grade levels, the meeting will more than likely focus on determining how to meet the needs of the 15–20% of the student population who need additional support to profit from the instructional core and meet grade-level expectations. That is, taking Path 2, they will identify those readers whose needs are unlike those of their peers in type (a few students persistently struggling to read words) or severity. These students will receive additional interventions, but this will take careful planning, informed by assessment results. As discussed in more detail below, some children will receive 30 minutes of support three times each week, while others, who need more intensive instruction, will meet with a specialist four times per week. These children will be reassessed every few weeks and the instruction they are receiving will be appropriately adjusted.

THE DECISION TREE IN LINGUISTICALLY DIVERSE SCHOOLS

When walking Path 2, schools should keep in mind that linguistically diverse students are referred to special education services far too often, a practice that is problematic because special education is meant for only a small percentage of this population—children whose difficulties run well beyond the challenge of learning English and literacy skills simultaneously. These children are not good candidates for special education, but they do benefit from rich day-to-day instruction and the opportunity to be exposed to language and concepts in small-group settings, where they can pose questions and practice using this language themselves. A helpful idea to keep in mind when examining a school's data is that learning difficulties, like those that can be addressed in special education, should be equally distributed in the population—7–12% of the population on average by most estimates (National Center for Education Statistics, 2009; Peña et al., 2011; Rodriguez et al., 2014). For these reasons, using the decision tree—an organizing structure for linking data to instruction—in the high-needs school setting is an especially important starting place for designing advanced literacy instruction.

The team will use specific cases to help anchor the planning discussion. Take, for example, Dexter. He's a second grader and AAE speaker, whose entry in the database provides an ample record of his unusual struggles with reading. Dexter appears to have poor phonemic decoding skills in comparison to his peers (as assessed by the Test of Word Reading Efficiency [TOWRE-2]) and struggles to read connected text fluently. When Dexter's teacher and the reading specialist received the results from the midyear testing cycle and went through the routine steps of understanding Dexter's individual profile as a learner, they planned a 6-week cycle of small-group instruction (Tier 2 support in a response to intervention or RTI framework) provided by the school's reading specialist. She met twice each week for 30 minutes with this small group to explicitly and systematically teach phonics skills. Through engaging word sorts and word work, opportunities to read and reread leveled text, and sight-word review, this instruction served as a "double dose" because Dexter continued to participate in the daily, high-quality classroom instruction focused on phonics and reading skills that he had been receiving. Dexter is not alone. Other children will receive additional support in mastering word-reading skills, while still others will work with a small group of peers and a teacher to gain additional exposure to the language and ideas contained in text. After a 6-week cycle, Dexter will be reevaluated and his supports adjusted accordingly (see Figure 5.8).

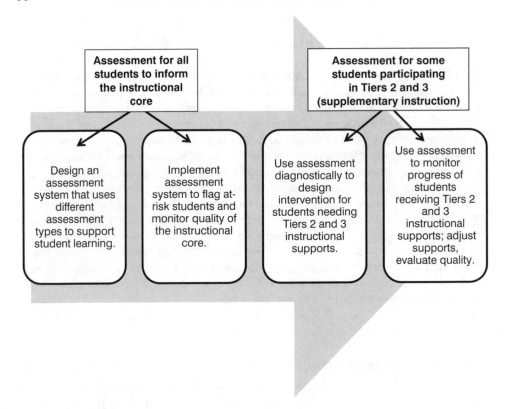

FIGURE 5.8. Linking assessment data to instructional tiers.

Action Step 4: Facilitate a Data-Centered Discussion Using the Decision Tree

Once you have completed Action Steps 1–3, use Leader's Tool 5.2 in the Appendix to identify trends and patterns in your data and formulate an instructional response. Data collected using Leader's Tools 4.1, 6.1, and 7.1 can augment your discussion of potential responses involving curriculum, professional development, and the allocation of instructional time.

Conclusions

In this chapter, we have taken on the topic of assessment, and provided an "express" version for leaders. To be sure, we've not exhausted this topic and we refer readers to our prior text, *Making Assessment Matter*, for additional information on the topic. Despite its brevity, this chapter offers an introduction to our vision for 21st-century assessment that attempts to recursively link data to instruction, resulting in a stronger core of instruction. In the chapters that follow, drawing on our experiences guiding schools to walk Path 1 of the decision tree, we focus on strengthening aspects of the instructional day that commonly come up short. In particular, we highlight how schools might better support the development of advanced literacy skills via adjustments to the curriculum and professional learning provided at the site. It is not surprising that many schools are struggling to deliver this type of instruction. After all, we are redefining what it means to be literate in today's society, and even instructional approaches that served children well in decades past are no longer enough to prepare them for the types of reading, writing, and speaking that we expect from them today. Luckily, the research on teaching and learning sheds light on how to provide this instruction and informs the recommendations for teaching advanced literacy that we unpack in Chapters 6 and 7.

APPENDIX 5.1. Native Language Assessment and Assessing Newcomers

Native Language Assessment

As we aim to better serve ELs in bilingual education settings and ensure that we are capturing their strengths, in many cases we revert to the idea that native language assessment is a good idea. When is literacy assessment in the native language a good idea?

1. If literacy instruction *is* in the native language, then assessment should be in the native language.
2. When instruction is not in the native language, the answer to this question becomes more complicated. Sometimes this can be an informative strategy, but it takes *sound professional judgment* in administering and interpreting the results of these assessments.

Here are some considerations about native language assessment for ELs who are receiving their instruction in English:

- The primary uses of assessment information in the native language is to guide instructional planning and supports and support student improvement; it should not be used to make high-stakes decisions.
  - There may be instances where it is helpful to know what a child knows in the native language and use this knowledge to "bridge" to English instruction.
- Native language assessments with external benchmarks were most often

designed for and normed on monolingual samples, receiving all instruction in the language of the assessment (e.g., learners in Puerto Rico).
  ▪ Scores for U.S. ELs must be interpreted accordingly.
• As students acquire a second language, one language may be more dominant because they are using that language more than the other at a particular point in time. Frequently children demonstrate a *language imbalance* as they progress toward bilingualism. During this time, children *may not perform as well* as native speakers in *either* language.
  ▪ This is a normal and most often temporary phase of emergent bilingualism.
• Many ELs in the United States, especially Spanish-speaking children, are also behind in their native language abilities because they are growing up in poverty, which influences their language-learning opportunities.

Assessment: What about Newcomers?

Newcomers are a special subgroup within the EL population. They are recent arrivals to the United States. Some will be new to formal schooling entirely and face the task of acquiring both a novel language and new content; whereas others, who have participated in formal schooling in their home countries, will face the challenge of translating content knowledge acquired in their native language into English. For all newcomers, oral and written assessments will guide a support plan.

Where Do Our Schoolwide Assessment Practices Fit In?

This will depend upon how and where the newcomer student is served. If the newcomer is being served in a classroom with nonnewcomer peers, and there is an assessment system in place, then once the student has sufficient proficiency to take the assessments, this student should be assessed. These assessments may provide helpful information, especially if administered over time, to support instructional planning. Within newcomer programs, assessments should be used to monitor progress, and many of the principles of data-driven assessments apply, but this is not a setting for a formal English literacy assessment.

CHAPTER 6

Using a Shared Curriculum or Platform to Support Daily Teaching and Learning

Once assessment data has been analyzed and trends and patterns identified in students' skills and competencies (see Chapter 5) and sites have taken stock of their needs and priorities with respect to teaching and professional development (Chapter 7), the work of tailoring the instructional core begins—our third key shift as introduced in Chapter 3. To undertake this curriculum design, leaders often look to the individuals in school buildings who bring the most expertise: teachers. But what this means in practical terms is that across the nation, each day, teachers are scrambling to both *design* and *deliver* curricula without the time to do so and, as a result, have limited energy to focus on students' learning needs.

The problem with turning teachers into curricula designers is that it fails to acknowledge the fact that teachers are *already* tasked with the delivery of instruction each day. They are busy creating interactive formats that promote content mastery, creating instructional groupings and engaging in formative assessment to determine when to reteach or move on. In today's typical classroom—one serving students with a range of needs: students acquiring English as a second language, students with disabilities, and students performing at grade level—this is a significant job in and of itself. Creating the classroom conditions where each learner is able to access grade-level materials and content is an ongoing process—one that often involves work with small groups, frequent reteaching, and ongoing assessment. To design curricula—to locate all of the materials to produce text sets that meet the needs of diverse groups, select learning protocols to teach, create assignments, and design assessments—requires much more time. In most cases, it demands time that the vast majority of teachers do not have built into their teaching day. It also demands a skill set or expertise that many teachers don't in fact possess (Huizinga, Handelzalts, Nieveen, & Voogt, 2015).

One might ask: What makes designing curricula so time-intensive? And wouldn't the very teachers who are closest to the students be best positioned to do this work? Well, curriculum design isn't just about creating daily lessons; it's also about designing a long-term plan for teaching and learning. Envisioning curriculum design this way has research findings at its core: we know that it takes multiple, varied learning opportunities to build advanced literacies skills, across time and different contexts, so our teaching must be "cumulative" and "coherent" (Hirsch & Hansel, 2013; Taylor et al., 2015). In other words, we need to engineer curricula so that students are exposed to learning opportunities that strike a fine balance between strategic redundancy and repetition and new tasks and routines, across skills and domains that often have a specific developmental progression. The curriculum must be aligned not only across the academic year but also vertically across the grades, a process that demands an extremely heavy investment of collaborative planning time. A single teacher working alone could not accomplish this alignment (Huizinga et al., 2015). Even a group of teachers working together would struggle to create a vertically and horizontally aligned core curriculum without sufficient time, resources, and consultative expertise—an unlikely combination in today's climate (Huizinga, Handelzalts, Nieveen, & Voogt, 2014).

In sum, we cannot assume that educators are properly supported to do this work, in addition to delivering instruction. To assume they could simultaneously fulfill the lesson-planning/teaching role while meanwhile engineering curricula is a recipe for unhappy consequences—for students, for teachers, and for the school as a whole. For students it means disjointed learning experiences from classroom to classroom as well as missed opportunities for deeper content learning. For teachers, it is a major contributing factor to burnout and turnover. For schools, it means no consistent plan for teaching and learning, and therefore the lack of a shared language around instruction. So, the central question becomes: How can we support teachers and provide the coherent and cohesive curriculum that students need?

Organization of This Chapter

To get to advanced literacies for all, we advocate for the implementation of a core curriculum—a shared platform for teaching and learning—as a central support for students and educators. This can consist of a high-quality packaged curriculum, one that is district-designed, or in cases where adequate

SITE-BASED CURRICULUM DESIGN: A CAUTIONARY TALE

Designing curricula at school sites can be a risky undertaking, especially in schools with high numbers of linguistically diverse and/or struggling readers. Why is this? Well, in these settings often the curriculum design is so tailored to the needs of students that we do not select materials that are on grade level. Over time, this can lead to a scenario where the first time students encounter grade-level materials and expectations are on a state test.

resources are available (time, finances, and a staff with adequate knowledge of curriculum design), a curriculum designed at the school site.

In the sections that follow, we highlight the benefits of curriculum—often a tough sell to educators from settings where curricula has been positioned not as a support but as a replacement for teacher expertise in instructional delivery. We then enumerate the characteristics of high-quality curricula, which, from our perspective, provides a shared platform to make the hallmarks of advanced literacies instruction explained in Chapter 4 a reality in classrooms. To support leaders in evaluating curricula, we share a checklist (Leader's Tool 6.1 in the Appendix). Finally, we introduce a framework for systematically adopting and adapting high-quality curricula at school sites to meet the needs of the population and, through a vignette, bring to life the process of implementing a specific curriculum at a school site, which necessarily includes adaptations (Woods, Dooley, Luke, & Exley, 2014).

What Are the Benefits of Curricula
for Students, Teachers, and Schools?

The curriculum is a key mechanism for creating high-quality literacy learning environments and a coordinated approach to instruction, with benefits for students, teachers, and the overall learning environment.

Benefits for Students

For students, a curriculum means learning tasks that become familiar and predictable in the face of changing content. It also means instructional language and skill-building goals that support advanced literacies development. From classroom to classroom this creates many instructional opportunities for students to work toward mastery (see Chapter 5).

Benefits for Teachers

For teachers, the benefits may be less apparent. In the past, curricula and teaching have often been confused; today we recognize that high-quality plans and materials are not a substitute for high-quality teachers. In addition, we've all been privy to circumstances that do in fact make the curriculum more a part of the problem than a part of an improvement effort (see Figure 6.1). In settings where the curriculum is put into place without any training or professional development structures and when it is used as a compliance mechanism (e.g., when pacing guides become a replacement for teacher expertise and judgment in instructional delivery), the curriculum likely does more harm than good. But in settings where the curriculum is present with effective supports and trainings, teachers can assume the primary role that teacher training prepares them for: to deliver instruction.

In these settings with effective supports and trainings, the curriculum becomes an important tool. It provides a starting place from which teachers can plan instructional delivery. And its presence frees up time that would otherwise be used for locating curricular materials to focus on designing and

Outdated Guiding Assumptions and Principles	21st-Century Realities and Guiding Principles
• Educators have enough time during the instructional day and during their planning time to find high-quality materials and design lessons that add up to a long-term plan for learning. • A curriculum is not a teaching support. • A curriculum deprofessionalizes teaching. • Standard training and professional development has supported teachers to be able to design curriculum.	• The little planning time that teachers do have should be spent focusing on planning for the implementation of differentiated instruction. • Having a well-designed, high-quality core curriculum in place acknowledges the teacher's primary role as an expert in instructional delivery. • Research demonstrates that a high-quality curriculum is a professional tool that contributes to daily on-the-job learning. ▪ Promotes subject-matter knowledge and content-based pedagogical knowledge. • Many teachers struggle to design a high-quality, aligned curriculum to promote knowledge-based literacy development across the year.

FIGURE 6.1. Capturing the context of Key Shift 3.

differentiating instruction for linguistically diverse students, many of whom need a significant boost academically. Because today's high-quality curricula most often take the latest research in teaching and learning and translate it for classroom application, interacting with current, high-quality materials provides teachers with ongoing, practice-embedded professional learning (Taylor et al., 2015). These high-quality plans and materials designed to promote student learning and teacher learning are what Davis and Krajcik (2005) have referred to as "educative curriculum"—they can bolster a teacher's subject-matter knowledge, pedagogical knowledge (e.g., how to teach vocabulary and support discussions), and pedagogical content knowledge for disciplinary practices (e.g., how to teach the scientific method). In other words, *the curriculum can become a tool for daily, on-the-job learning.*

You can verify this with the teachers themselves, as we found in working to implement an academic vocabulary curriculum for middle grades. We saw in participating teachers' implementation logs and end-of-implementation interviews that the curriculum itself was a central support. In fact, during the interviews, when asked to choose the essential component from a list of supports we provided (curriculum, coaching, monthly meetings with colleagues using the curriculum) to make the initiative a success, one teacher answered, "The curriculum. Because when it comes down to it, it's you, the classroom, and the curriculum. And so that's the biggest piece of support." Some teachers also found that the curriculum provided support for their content-knowledge development. One teacher explained how plans and materials boosted her knowledge base: "To be honest, I always get 'affect' and 'effect' mixed up. This lesson actually helped me with it" (Lesaux et al., 2010).

Of particular interest to us were teachers' comments and impressions about scripted lessons, which were included in the curriculum as optional models—either to use in preparation, to use while teaching, or not to use at all. While we as a field have been engaged in an ongoing conversation around the utility of scripted curricula, teachers suggested that these explicit lessons were helpful. One teacher wrote, "Honestly, the fact that I had the binder with the scripted lesson and the outline—that was all the support I needed. I didn't need anything else." Several teachers indicated that they thought this type of instructional model was most beneficial to new teachers. Specifically, the teachers who reported that they relied heavily on the models during the early stages of implementation and later used them as a reference, picking and choosing ideas and examples, each had less than 4 years' teaching experience. As one teacher reported, "Quite frankly, I started out using all the scripted lessons. But as I got more comfortable, then I would do my own or change a little bit here and there, you know, change it around. Because you gotta have that teacher comfortableness with it."

Benefits for Schools

Beyond the benefits for students and teachers, there are benefits of a high-quality curriculum at the level of the classroom- and school-learning environments. These benefits include (Squires, 2009):

- Having a shared set of pedagogical practices from classroom to classroom.
- Enhanced classroom management practices (e.g., behavior and time management) and quality of interactions.
- Developmentally appropriate pacing that promotes student engagement and on-task behaviors.
- Literacy-rich materials (libraries, posters, props, etc.) that are familiar to all teachers and students, and that support a cohesive learning experience.

For instance, teachers involved in the curricular initiative we just mentioned told us that working with other adults around a shared curricular platform had unexpected positive consequences. Although formal collaboration was not required, teachers frequently worked together to decide how to deliver curricular content or, as one teacher put it, they worked on "debugging" the program. Discussions included sharing ideas for classroom arrangements and supplemental materials. While the curriculum didn't aim to create a community of practice, this was exactly what happened at many school sites. Last but certainly not least, formal professional development opportunities and structures that use a shared language and revolve around a shared set of practices and knowledge-building goals support and promote a culture of excellence around instruction.

What Makes a Curriculum "High Quality"?

While we cannot confuse curriculum materials with good teaching, we can support good teaching by providing educators with high-quality, comprehensive curricular materials. High-quality literacy curricula have all of these characteristics:

1. The hallmarks of advanced literacies instruction are present in all lessons and across units (see Chapter 4).
2. Tasks and texts provided in the curriculum are appropriately challenging given grade-level standards and thus support holding all students, including linguistically diverse students, to high expectations.
3. The curricular sequence has been designed to provide ample instructional opportunities to develop target skills and competencies.
4. Supports for linguistically diverse learners (and other types of learners) are explicit throughout, including suggestions for adaptations of tasks and materials for ELs and nonmainstream dialect speakers.
5. To support fidelity of implementation, lesson plans provide adequate detail to execute lessons as designed and teachers are provided with all corresponding materials.
6. The curriculum serves an educative function by providing teachers a rationale for the design of each activity and task.

To support leaders and their teams in evaluating the quality of a site's curriculum plans and materials, or in selecting or leading the designing of curriculum that meet this criteria, we have provided Leader's Tool 6.1 in the Appendix. Our suggestion to leaders and their teams engaged in selection of a new curriculum is this: Use this checklist in an open, transparent process as you cross-compare two or three curricula before choosing the one you will implement. This information should then be shared with the larger faculty. By making the process transparent, faculty who were not on the selection committee are aided in understanding the rationale that guided the curriculum's selection.

Implementing and Adapting Curricula: A Road Map

After a high-quality curriculum has been designed and created, or purchased, the real work begins—the work that determines whether the curriculum will be beneficial as part of the improvement effort or yet another initiative that doesn't gain enough traction to make a difference. All too often, it is the latter—sites may have a very strong curriculum at their fingertips but the initiative fails because of lack of attention to careful, supported, and deep implementation. This is why we view the adoption of a new curriculum to be a multiyear process that follows two phases: a pilot[1] and a full-scale implementation phase. In both phases, the curriculum may be adapted following a systematic process, explained below, that ensures a level of fidelity.[2]

In our work with dozens of partner schools, we hear all too often from teachers that the curriculum "did not work" after a year of implementation. But often this follows a year where we have observed one of two tendencies due to lack of a school-based implementation plan: (1) adopting a new curriculum and *immediately* beginning to adapt it to meet the needs of the student population; (2) adopting a new curriculum and simply picking and choosing which aspects will be implemented. We advocate strongly against both approaches, although it is perhaps less obvious why the first tendency is a problem. Ultimately, in both cases, each teacher is implementing a different curriculum altogether from classroom to classroom. Most often, their decisions about adaptations and selections for teaching are more idiosyncratic than they are strategic. They tend to be inspired by more or less familiarity and preference with certain aspects than by perceived student needs. At many schools, we have seen this perception—that the curriculum has not been successful—lead to it being abandoned in favor of another curriculum or approach. For educators and administrators, this constant cycle of repeatedly adopting and abandoning curricula is taxing professionally, and costly with respect to resources (e.g., time, money) and effects on learner outcomes. Here, we describe the pilot phase and a full-scale implementation phase, which together make for a 2-year process.

Phase 1: The Pilot Phase

During the pilot phase, a small group of teachers volunteer to be "early adopters." These teachers should be representative of all end users and committed to a genuine pilot process. Often these teams are comprised of a teacher in each grade, or half of a content-area faculty. Asked to implement the curriculum *as it is written* for 1 academic year, these early adopters collect data throughout the year (e.g., which topics required reteaching after being taught

---

[1] At schools where the curriculum is being designed on site, the pilot phase should follow a design phase in which teachers work as a team to create the curriculum. This design phase can occur during the academic year and/or the summer before the pilot.

[2] Often "fidelity" is interpreted as slavish dedication to a curriculum that may not be serving students. This is not what we mean. Instead, fidelity refers to teaching of lessons initially as written and then reteaching making adaptations if necessary.

using the lessons provided, which texts required the use of supplementary texts and materials for struggling readers) and eventually offer feedback on its general fit with students' needs and its ease of implementation. They then work with leadership to plan the implementation at scale the subsequent year—informing strategic adaptations and an implementation plan, including professional development supports. This *adaptation process* brings together early adopters in grade-level or content-area teams to make decisions about *which* aspects of the curriculum to adapt and *how* to go about adapting them. The team should document the changes made to the curriculum and note why. Decisions should be based on data from teacher logs or observation notes.

We are often asked why we suggest teachers initially teach the curriculum as written. Our answer is that it takes more than one solid trial to get to know and become familiar with a curriculum, working through the kinks and discomfort of the early days. Without that lengthy trial it is difficult to step back and reflect upon the fit between the curriculum, the students, and the teaching context, and to troubleshoot around tweaks and adaptations, etc. (Yurdakula, 2015). We know, for example, that the feedback on a curriculum in its first 6 or 8 weeks of implementation is most often not at all representative of—or the same as—the feedback that same teacher has at the end of year 1 of implementation.

Note that we are *not* suggesting that fidelity of implementation is the same as adhering to a curriculum as written. After all, as designed, no curriculum meets the needs of all learners and in settings serving high numbers of linguistically diverse learners, this is certainly rarely the case. What we mean to suggest is an approach that is strategic about modifications and adaptations, whether they affect pacing or the scope and sequence of lessons within the overarching plan. On that basis, the team can proceed with redesigning the curriculum and implementation accordingly, creating a data-driven adaptation—and implementing that with fidelity. In sum, leaders need a systematic approach for making necessary adaptations to support ELs and their peers. It can be appealing to allow each educator to make these decisions for his or her own students, but this is a strategy that can quickly create very different instructional conditions in all classrooms and undermine our ability to assess whether a curriculum is effective.

If adaptations must be made, we suggest adhering to the guidelines in Figure 6.2. Beyond the practical and professional benefits, a pilot often builds excitement and interest around a new instructional initiative, making others eager to participate and receive the additional resources.

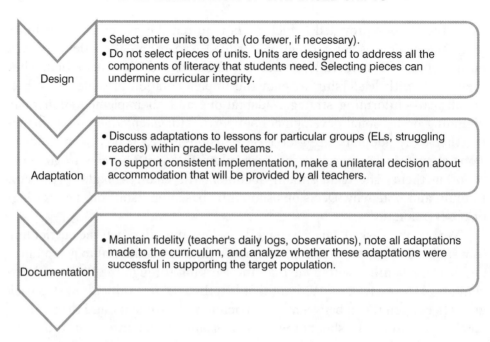

FIGURE 6.2. Guidelines for curriculum design and adaptation.

Phase 2: Full-Scale Implementation

Once a curriculum has been successfully piloted over 1 academic year, it can be rolled out in all classrooms. The team of teachers who served as early adopters are central to the rollout, guiding other teachers as they implement the new curriculum. During the full-scale implementation phase, adaptations may still need to be made to the curriculum. Again, the process described above should be used to ensure that changes made to the curriculum are implemented in the same way across classrooms.

What Does 21st-Century Curriculum Implementation Look Like?

It is the end of August and the middle school staff of the Rosa Parks School has gathered for its yearly summer institute. Despite nearly 90-degree temperatures and cramped conditions in the lunchroom, the sixth- to eighth-grade faculty is excited to discuss the rollout of a new literacy curriculum. They are following the same process the school has used to select and implement new math and social studies curricula over the last 18 months. It began with a small committee of volunteers—teachers from each grade level, literacy specialists, and

Principal Lansdowne—reviewing a number of curricula and finally selecting one that met their criteria. The chosen curriculum was then piloted in six of the 12 classrooms in the middle school—two in sixth grade, two in seventh grade, and two in eighth grade.

One faculty member volunteering for the pilot, sixth-grade teacher Rosie Martinez, had been anxious about the pilot process that Principal Lansdowne had described. Many of this teacher's students were second language learners and she had never been asked to teach lessons as outlined in a teacher's edition *before* making any adaptations. Typically, her first step when teaching from a curriculum has been to select only those activities that she considered suitable, based on student need, while disregarding the others. In what had been an uncomfortable meeting with Principal Lansdowne, Ms. Martinez was resistant: *What if her students failed? What if they struggled too much?*

Despite her initial reaction, she had agreed to give it a try. Principal Lansdowne made a strong case for exposing her students to varying levels of text and tasks and for systematically documenting where the curriculum could be improved to make grade-level texts accessible to all students. She would teach the lessons as described in the teacher's edition of the new curriculum and take notes about what felt successful and what didn't—and then discuss these impressions, using her logs, in meetings with the other early adopters during a weekly block set aside by Principal Lansdowne. The group would discuss the adaptations they were inclined to make to particular lessons when they retaught them to the few students (or sometimes the entire class) who needed additional support. Sometimes, the group would work together to find a supplementary text, materials (e.g., videos) that could be used to build background knowledge, or brainstorm a new way to explain a concept. Then they would return to their classrooms and implement the lesson with the planned adaptations and modifications. And the cycle would repeat itself.

A few things had surprised Ms. Martinez about the pilot process. First, her students were more successful reading grade-level materials than she had anticipated. She was also surprised by how helpful she had found the peer collaboration; during the weekly meeting, her colleagues often had suggestions about adapting the curriculum that she wouldn't have considered. Finally, the curriculum, even though it wasn't perfect, had taught her some new teaching tricks and because of those and the curriculum's plans she noticed that she had more time to consider new ways to assess student's developing knowledge of language and concepts. While she had traditionally administered an end-of-unit assessment, this year she also introduced oral exams and capstone projects as formats for students to demonstrate their understanding and emerging mastery of key concepts.

Today, at the summer institute, Ms. Martinez was leading a small group of her sixth-grade colleagues through the curriculum. She was surprised by how much she knew and how comfortable she felt. At first, she had spent hours reading the curriculum to prepare to teach, but as the pilot year wore on, she was gradually able to lead the weekly meetings with ease—discussing implementation successes and troubleshooting challenges. She knew that many of her colleagues' classrooms looked different from hers and that they would need support in making strategic adaptations. Principal Lansdowne had made a commitment to the faculty to continue to use this curriculum for at least 5 years; Rosie Martinez and her colleagues knew that the next year would be time well spent.

Taking Action: Implementing Key Shift 3

Action Step 1: Defining Evaluation Criteria and Selecting a High-Quality Curriculum

Evaluating the quality of current curricular plans and materials in place at a school site or selecting a new curriculum to implement involves establishing a set of criteria for what constitutes high-quality instructional plans and materials. In the Appendix, we provide a checklist (Leader's Tool 6.1) that can be used for this purpose. However, given the goals of a particular school site (core mission, instructional focus), leaders may wish to add additional criteria to those provided in Leader's Tool 6.1.

Action Step 2: Adopting and Adapting a High-Quality Curriculum

If a site has opted to implement a new curriculum, the steps outlined above (from pilot to full-scale implementation) should be followed and the adaptation cycle repeated as often as necessary in the first few years.

Indicators of Successful Implementation

The approach we suggest in this chapter—that of selecting a high-quality curriculum and then sticking with it over many curricular cycles, focusing only on slight adaptations to fit the context—requires a leadership team that is committed to "staying the course," even as new instructional models, materials, and programs are adopted by the district. This approach runs counter to

- Students' learning opportunities are more consistent and cohesive from classroom to classroom and from grade to grade.
- Teachers feel more supported with respect to availability of teaching tools.
- There is a shared language at the site around instructional content and routines.
  - Supports more specific conversations about differentiated approach to the instructional core.
- Curriculum is a key mechanism for onboarding new faculty; supports smooth transition.

FIGURE 6.3. Key Shift 3: Target outcomes.

the status quo, which tends to involve short cycles of adoption and discontinuance followed by a new initiative or program, but for school sites that invest in a long-term plan for teaching and learning, we can anticipate the outcomes shown in Figure 6.3.

As we discussed, designing and creating or purchasing a high-quality curriculum for a school site and making its materials available to all teachers is likely to have very little impact if we do not also attend to the corresponding professional learning that needs to occur as part of the implementation process. Whether it's a new curriculum or the introduction of a new instructional practice, the success of any improvement initiative depends directly upon the quality of the corresponding training and support that is offered. Therefore, in the following chapter, we turn to the final shift central to promoting advanced literacies at school sites—creating the context for 21st-century adult learning.

CHAPTER 7

Leading the Implementation of Sustained Approaches to Staff Development

Getting to a new model of instruction to promote advanced literacies for all students will require a new model for leading instructional change (Key Shift 4, Chapter 3). As in any profession, the importance of continually transforming educators' knowledge—in this case about learning and teaching—cannot be understated. Their practice in classrooms will flow directly from what they learn. It is well documented that leaders can have a powerful influence on students' literacy. This influence is indirect, however, because it is tied up in how well leaders organize the setting for instructional improvement and support those who are in daily learning and teaching roles (Waters, Marzano, & McNulty, 2003). Given that knowledge is not institutionalized—that excellence resides in the individuals in the organization—educators (teachers, literacy and second language specialists, and paraprofessionals) at school sites are the key mechanism through which services, supports, and interventions promote development and learning. For example, in a 6-year longitudinal study of the impact of school-related factors on students' outcomes in 180 schools, only teaching exerted a greater influence than leadership (Leithwood, Louis, Wahlstrom, & Anderson, 2010). In summary, achieving universal advanced literacies for all students comes down to the quality of the instructional leadership and teaching.

Taking today's standards and literacy demands seriously, there's no question that we are asking our teachers to teach differently. In many cases, we are asking educators to teach skills and competencies that were not in focus during their formal training. For example, promoting our students' advanced literacies requires the creation of classrooms where students are speaking, reading, and writing more than ever before. Also, in today's classrooms, and in particular in linguistically diverse settings, teachers must craft the language environment with greater intentionality to increase the amount and quality of language produced, by teachers and students alike. And in so doing, we are asking content-area teachers—many of whom have no formal training in literacy development or second language development—to attend to the inter-relatedness of content knowledge development and advanced literacies. At the same time, in settings serving high numbers of linguistically diverse students, teachers more often than not have doubts about whether they are meeting students' needs and have many questions about strategies, approaches, and materials that would best support their students.

For leaders, many of whom are under pressure to raise literacy rates and who are already spending significant amounts of time and money on programs and training, this means a different route to supporting teachers to grow as practitioners. To support teachers to design the instructional opportunities and learning environments of today, leaders must create 21st-century adult learning opportunities at school sites. This often means making substantive changes to our adult learning environment (Figure 7.1). To that end, today's leaders ask many questions: *What models of professional development are effective? How can we make professional learning more meaningful and impactful? Which literacy skills and competencies should we be focusing on?*

Organization of This Chapter

In this chapter, we provide guidance to leaders looking to create and offer professional learning that leads to classroom environments that support advanced literacy. We point out the need to change the traditional approach to adult learning in two significant ways: (1) to bring the *format* of professional learning up to date with what we know about adult learning and transforming practice; and (2) to update the *substance* of professional learning to match today's literacy demands and the literacy needs of our linguistically diverse population. In addressing the first goal, we feature two structures—professional learning communities (PLCs) and connected coaching—which, when implemented effectively, are concrete examples of 21st-century approaches to professional development that fit today's context. At the close of this chapter, we provide a window into what the continuous cycle and its structures look like in practice at the Rosa Parks School.

Outdated Guiding Principles and Practices	21st-Century Realities and Guiding Principles

• Specific topics of professional interest (e.g., strategies for teaching ELs; leading discussions in the upper elementary classroom) addressed independently will support improved practice in advanced literacies.
 	
• Brief, one-off sessions transform educator knowledge and practice about instruction to promote advanced literacies.
 	
• Individual teachers sign up for outside sessions based on their own interest(s) and professional needs—or their participation is mandated.
	• To promote advanced literacies for all, professional learning opportunities needs to have these characteristics:
	  ▪ Focused on a limited set of pedagogical strategies and approaches to build composite competencies (see Chapters 2 and 4), anchored in a knowledge-building plan for students and teachers.
	  ▪ Continuous, site-based work guided and refined on the basis of data (both student data and teacher data collected via observations).
	  ▪ Involves site-based teams made up of educators and instructional leaders with decision-making authority.
	  ▪ Opportunities for feedback on teaching and guided reflection on practice.
	
	• If off-site professional learning occurs, it is coupled with planned site-based follow-up and opportunities for classroom-based application and feedback.
	  ▪ Note: Off-site professional development offered by experts can be an excellent tool for launching a site-based initiative.

FIGURE 7.1. Capturing the context of Key Shift 4.

Updating the Format for Professional Learning

Just as we need to redesign our students' learning environments to get to deeper learning for advanced literacies, we must also redesign the way we promote learning and practice change among the adults charged with taking our classrooms to the next level. Today, many educators are not provided with sufficient or effective training opportunities to deliver on the goal of advanced literacies for all. For some, there is no training whatsoever; for others, the professional education they receive lacks sufficient intensity and relevance to gain traction in the practice setting. That is to say, even when professional development does occur, our current paradigm favors periodic training sessions that are relatively brief, one-size-fits-all, and disconnected from daily classroom practice. Trainings are typically short in duration (e.g., one-half or one full day) and maintain teacher isolation by having individuals participate alone rather than as school-based teams.

Finally, the knowledge gained in professional learning is often challenging to put into practice once teachers return to the classroom. Follow-up support, such as coaching, or participation in an intensive PLC that includes individuals who have observed each other teach and can offer guidance, is rarely offered (Darling-Hammond et al., 2009). But short of offering this kind of genuine learning process—one that provides sustained opportunities to apply and reflect upon emerging knowledge—we cannot expect the kinds of changes we're so often hoping for.

The adults in school buildings share at least one characteristic with all of their students: they too are all learners. Here, we encourage the reader to draw some parallels between what it will take to transform adults' knowledge and practice and what it will take to build up students' advanced literacies. For example, some studies demonstrate that, on average, teachers require at least 20 separate instances of in-context practice—with scaffolding and support— before a new skill is mastered. And if the skill or competency being taught is more complex (such as how to gradually build students' composite competencies, including the skill to synthesize a complex text), the number of instances of practice required increases (Joyce & Showers, 2002). Teachers often encounter difficulty when learning a new teaching technique, and command only comes by persevering through these awkward, often frustrating initial attempts. Without support, most teachers will not persevere. Therefore, whether receiving professional development over a series of sessions or work-

---

SHOULD PROFESSIONAL LEARNING ALWAYS BE ON-SITE?

Off-site professional learning, for many reasons, not the least of which is maximizing resources and creating opportunities for shared learning, is a very common structure and occurrence across the field. While some would advocate all professional development should be site-based, it is our experience that off-site professional development can be effective, under particular conditions:

- When it is coupled with planned site-based follow-up and opportunities for classroom-based application and feedback.
- When it is team-based and provides multiple sessions with work in between (e.g., much like a college or university course).
- When it serves as the launch or kick-off to a site-based initiative.

ing in a PLC at their school sites, teachers need to be applying new learnings in their own classrooms.

As leaders move forward in today's context of challenges and opportunities, we know that there are several characteristics related to the format of professional learning that must be present—in combination—for professional development to effect lasting, positive changes in the service of creating strong and successful learners. That is, to promote advanced literacies for all, professional learning opportunities must have these characteristics:

- Be continuous, involving site-based work that is guided and refined on the basis of data (both student data and teacher data).
- Be supported by site-based teams made up of educators and instructional leaders with decision-making authority.
- Be linked to opportunities for feedback on teaching and guided reflection on practice (via PLCs or connected coaching).

In turn, as shown in Figure 7.2, these characteristics form the basis for the cycle of continuous, site-level improvement that is at the core of adult learning and transformation in practice. At the close of this chapter, we provide a window into what this continuous cycle and its structures look like in practice at the Rosa Parks School.

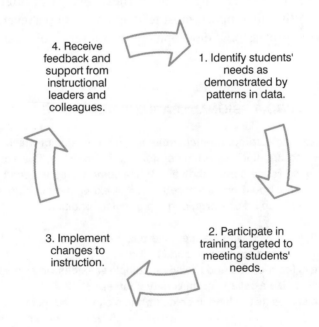

FIGURE 7.2. Continuous, site-level professional development.

Spotlight: PLCs and Connected Coaching

Within this cycle or process, we highlight two core structures that when implemented effectively are examples of approaches to 21st-century adult learning—PLCs and connected coaching—each of which are key supports for fostering the conditions for continuous improvement. PLCs involve groups of colleagues, including a skilled facilitator, who meet regularly to discuss and problem-solve around instructional practices that are central to the current improvement effort. Connected coaching can occur as a follow-up to the PLC in an informal manner—for example, by a PLC colleague who has experienced a struggle that another may be experiencing and/or who has ideas on how to troubleshoot and/or get to the next level. Most often, though, connected coaching involves a more formal format, bringing together an instructional expert (a coach) and a practitioner to analyze and reflect on a lesson or set of lessons that feature the key instructional practices in focus at the site as part of the improvement effort, with an eye toward boosting teaching and learning.[1] As shown in Figure 7.3, PLCs and connected coaching share "active ingredients."

Format	Approach to Knowledge Building	Mechanisms That Transform Practice
• Ongoing, part of a long-term plan for teaching and learning.	• Guided by an interest in fostering advanced literacies competencies. • Interactive, using discussion and dialogue. • Anchored in data (classroom visit, student work that can be collaboratively reflected on). • Assumes a nonjudgmental and responsive stance (is not linked to teacher evaluation or compliance).	• Provides opportunities to practice high-quality teaching and learning routines that support advanced literacies with built-in time for reflection and iteration. • Promotes problem solving and anticipation of roadblocks. • Encourages educators to struggle productively with new teaching and learning structures on the way to mastery.

FIGURE 7.3. Commonalities between PLCs and coaching.

---

[1] In our work focused on reading specialists and coaches, we have found that not all have received adequate support to develop the skills needed to serve as catalysts of schoolwide literacy reform efforts that link data to instruction (Galloway & Lesaux, 2015). In light of this challenge, we encourage leaders to provide professional learning opportunities to reading specialists and coaches to prepare them to take on these new roles.

Updating the Substance
of Professional Learning

As leaders move forward in today's context of challenges and opportunities, we know that beyond the characteristics related to the format of professional learning that must be present for professional development to effect lasting, positive changes in the service of creating strong and successful learners, the substance of the professional development must reflect today's literacy demands. All professional learning opportunities must increasingly be directed at equipping teachers with the know-how to develop students' advanced literacies. In practice this means that professional development must be:

- Focused on a limited set of pedagogical strategies and approaches designed to build a student's composite competencies (see Chapters 2 and 4), anchored in a knowledge-building plan for students and teachers.
- Linked to a specific, site-level need as surfaced by data (Peery, 2004), rather than on topics of general interest or reflecting educational fads.

PLCs and professional learning opportunities must therefore be guided by the goal of developing an understanding of the component skills and composite competencies that go into advanced literacies (see Chapter 2). A PLC might focus, for example, on what skills are involved in producing a persuasive essay in the upper elementary and middle grades and to analyze and agree upon— and then implement, test, and revise—a set of strategies to develop these competencies through instruction (see Chapter 4). Often this collaborative work around instructional plans and teaching, occurring in PLCs or other adult learning communities, is referred to as "lesson study" (Lewis, 2002). These discussions must be rooted in student achievement data that give insight into how the separable component skills that make up the composite competencies are developing in the student population and these data should be used to inform the design of day-to-day content-area instruction and intervention for students who are struggling (see Chapter 5). For that reason, they should also be connected to the curricular plans and materials (see Chapter 6). Because a focus on advanced literacies is relatively recent, school leaders must also be engaged in the complex work of supporting teachers to advance their existing practices, a process that begins with demonstrating to colleagues that this instruction will support their discipline-centric instructional goals (Murnane, Sharkey, & Boudett, 2005).

The Role of the Leader

At the same time, elevated student achievement is linked to instructional leadership. It has become clear that results improve when administrators spend significant time reviewing student data with teachers, monitoring and supporting curricular implementation, understanding instructional strategies tailored to the population at hand, and supporting problem solving, troubleshooting, and midcourse corrections in response to patterns in student data. Increasing the time leaders spend directly supporting instruction, and creating a culture of reflection and professional expertise, are key steps toward data-driven advanced literacy instruction.

What Does 21st-Century Professional Learning Look Like?

On Thursday afternoons, the 10 members of the eighth-grade teacher team meet as a PLC. This year marks the third year that Jayson Washington, eighth-grade teacher of ELs, has participated. The PLC is focused this year on increasing students' oral language production as a support for content and language learning (Hallmark 2, Chapter 4), a topical focus that was inspired by a professional development session that the entire PLC had attended together the previous fall. Today, Jayson Washington is presenting on a recent lesson in which he adapted accountable talk frames (a learning protocol used by all Rosa Parks School teachers; see Chapter 5 for a discussion of protocols) for his newcomer students. He and his colleagues are brainstorming ways to help students use these talk frames independently, which requires teaching his students to listen carefully to peers. Others in the group have struggled with helping students listen to others and to build on ideas that other students provide, to get past discussions that don't build to something greater. Jana Potter, an eighth-grade English language arts teacher, suggests the use of a talking stick or ball that the student can only pass if he or she has commented on another student's comments. Others nod and Mr. Washington agrees to try this strategy with his students. He will return next week to share the outcome and to brainstorm additional strategies. In the coming week, Jana Potter will visit his classroom to see if she can offer additional coaching strategies. This conversation has been helpful not only to Jayson—other teachers are facing the same struggles and likewise benefited from the session.

However, shifting to focus on academic talk has been a huge change in practice for Jayson Washington. While he used to focus on teaching more conversational language to his students first, participation in this PLC has helped

Mr. Washington recognize the set of academic language skills that his students will need to participate in all content-area classrooms, and which they are unlikely to acquire in day-to-day conversation with peers. Up until 3 years ago, Jayson Washington rarely attended professional learning that targeted middle school teachers. As one of two teachers of EL students at the Rosa Parks School, he attended professional learning, often provided by the district, that focused narrowly on this population; he could not have articulated the goals for all eighth graders at the school site. Working with his PLC had changed that and Mr. Washington now feels that he is part of something larger, a team that is making change. All over the school similar teams are at work. While meetings may occasionally be used to discuss particular learners, this is not the general purpose of the PLC; instead, these meetings are about moving teaching practice forward.

To support this work at the Rosa Parks School, Principal Lansdowne visits the PLCs on a regular basis during the Thursday meeting times that she has carved out. In the first year that PLCs met at Rosa Parks, all PLCs and all other school-based professional development sessions focused on a single topic: using student data to inform instruction (Key Shift 2, Chapter 5). Over the last 2 years, each grade-level PLC has focused on developing its advanced literacy pedagogical skills. Because improvement is incremental rather than sweeping, each team has a single, narrow focus. From grade to grade, each PLC is working on a different instructional hallmark (Chapter 4) based on the needs they've identified in grade-level student data. The sixth-grade team is focused on texts—locating a variety of texts and engaging in an ongoing inquiry around ways to support access to more complex texts for linguistically diverse learners. In contrast, the fourth-grade team is focusing on how to use extended writing as a tool to support content mastery across content areas. To support each PLC, Principal Lansdowne actively looks for district-provided opportunities that align with each PLC's area of focus. In addition, site-based professional learning often taps into the knowledge of teachers on staff. For instance, the sixth-grade team, which had worked extensively on advancing oral language skills in their classrooms last year, recently ran a professional development session for colleagues.

The choice to reboot the adult learning opportunities at Rosa Parks School was made after Principal Lansdowne had examined the quality of the initiatives in place and been dismayed to find that they lacked intensity, were on a range of somewhat disjointed topics, and were generally disliked by staff. That said, for Principal Lansdowne, creating PLCs was a drastic and unpopular shift—teachers were accustomed to choosing their own professional learning sessions and to them the weekly PLC format felt, at first, like a waste of time. However, 3 years into the initiative their efforts were bearing fruit. Classrooms looked and sounded different. They weren't the quiet, stand-and-deliver environments of years past. A recent walk-through by the superintendent and her leadership team had confirmed that the Rosa Parks School was on the right track.

Taking Action: Implementing Key Shift 4

Action Step 1: Inventory a Site's Current Professional Learning Landscape

To examine the formats for professional learning and the substance of a site's current adult-learning initiative, we have provided Leader's Tool 7.1 in the Appendix. This checklist can be used to understand the current opportunities for adult learners at a school site, and to plan for future professional learning.

Action Step 2: Adjusting Format and/or Substance of Professional Learning

Once areas for adjusting the format or substance of a site's professional learning have been identified, we suggest returning to the staff—either through a survey or town meeting—to discuss potential changes to format and substance. In this meeting, leaders and faculty should work collaboratively to identify a shared set of action steps and to be sure that the professional learning being offered will meet the faculty's needs.

Summary

For today's leaders, getting to advanced literacies for all students means starting with all educators involved in instruction in their building. It requires focusing on their ongoing professional learning: the timing and availability of professional learning opportunities, the school's resources dedicated to teacher learning, the substantive focus, and the school's collaborative climate. Elements of that climate would include the tenor of the interactions among teachers, between teachers and students, and within the professional community. They would also include the educational culture, such as the degree to which there are high expectations for students and an overall improve-

- A staff that embraces a growth mind-set and is guided by the principle that gaining command of new instructional strategies and knowledge takes time and requires ongoing practice.
- There is distributed leadership among the staff around the literacy improvement effort. It is not tied to one person and is sustained in the face of turnover and absences.
- Professional development plans that arise out of needs expressed by faculty or student data.
  - Strict adherence to subscribing only to those opportunities that are central to the improvement agenda.

FIGURE 7.4. Key Shift 4: Target outcomes.

ment orientation (Desimone, Porter, Garet, Yoon, & Birman, 2002; Louis, Leithwood, Walhstrom, & Anderson, 2010). As shown in Figure 7.4, in schools where 21st-century learning is underway, there are a number of characteristics we see regularly: we typically meet a highly collaborative staff that embraces a growth mind-set—they are in the habit of ongoing practice and discussion about priority instructional techniques. Problems and challenges and professional development topics arise out of needs uncovered by data that is focused on the development of advanced literacies, primarily composite competencies (see Chapter 2).

PART III

Moving Forward at a School Site

CHAPTER 8

Bringing It All Together

Generating a Blueprint for Advanced Literacies Instruction

It is September, and Principal Lansdowne stands at her office window watching parents and caregivers as they deliver their newly minted kindergarteners—some clearly excited, others clearly cautious—into the capable hands of teachers Jane Walker and Jim Huang. She observes as one mother stoops to kiss the top of her son's head and releases his small hand from hers. After a moment, Principal Lansdowne recognizes him as Miguel, a kindergartener whom she met during last week's kindergarten orientation. Miguel looks excited as he marches into the classroom, small red backpack and Superman lunchbox in hand. His mother stands watching, her face conveying a mix of anxiety and pride as she waves goodbye to her little boy—but he hardly seems to notice.

For Miguel and for many children and their families at the school, this marks their first interaction with the U.S. education system. Like all parents, Miguel's mother has many hopes and aspirations for his future, all of which are shared by Principal Lansdowne and her team. Nonetheless, preparing Miguel and all of Rosa Parks's students for the rapidly changing global economy, one in which basic literacy skills are no longer enough, is a humbling responsibility and not without challenges—or, as Principal Lansdowne was always reminding her faculty, opportunities.

This year, Principal Lansdowne is feeling particularly optimistic; it is the start of the fourth year of a comprehensive effort to create the classroom conditions where advanced literacies for all students are possible. It's certainly not been an easy journey; Principal Lansdowne had spent the first year of the initiative—filled with difficult conversations and long hours—doubting whether their time and effort would pay off. And actually, at the end of that year, they had very little tangible evidence that their efforts were having any impact; their students' test scores remained low even when compared to other schools in their large urban district. In the time since, however, their collective efforts have started to produce results; in the last 2 years they've seen a reduction in literacy-related difficulties that demand intervention and a decrease in special education referrals, especially among their large and growing population of linguistically diverse learners. An instructional model that strives to build knowledge and language was a shift from the traditional model at the Rosa Parks School, but this seemed to be exactly the approach needed to support the school's ELs.

While August typically involved a flurry of teacher hiring, this year was different. For the first time in many years, the school is retaining more teachers as a result of the leadership team's efforts to provide key supports (a core curriculum and ongoing professional learning) to the adult learners in the building. Intangible results from this ongoing effort have been numerous—more collaboration between grade-level teaching teams, the instruction in each classroom "looks" and "feels" more similar across the school, and there is an energy in the school—an excitement—about what is possible for its students.

Revisiting the Context of Leading Advanced Literacies Instruction

There is no question that Principal Lansdowne and her staff are involved in the hardest work to be found throughout the education system. At the Rosa Parks School and across the nation, the press for universal advanced literacies recognizes the new role that language and literacy skills play in our knowledge-based society, both in our neighborhoods and in the world at large. Today's students need to develop an increasingly complex set of advanced literacy skills and competencies in order to access social and economic opportunities. Importantly, as we discussed in the opening chapter of this book, the press for advanced literacies for all does not reflect a decline in the population's literacy rates. Instead it is recognition that what counts as "literate" has changed dramatically over the last few decades (Murnane & Levy, 2005).

This press for advanced literacies skills and competencies comes at a time when our schools are become more linguistically diverse places; greater numbers of students in our classrooms are acquiring academic English for the first time upon school entry, with the most significant growth in the school-age population of ELs occurring in our secondary schools (Garcia & Cuéllar, 2006). This growth will likely continue; by 2030, it is anticipated that 40%

of the U.S. school-age population will speak a language other than English at home (Camarota, 2012). Also, many students other than those formally classified as ELs are learning English as an additional language. Even if not in the initial stages of language development, these children are often described as "language-minority learners." Likewise, there are ever more students who speak a nonmainstream dialect of English that is different from the academic English found in school curricula in schools across the United States (Washington et al., 2013).[1] While it is easy to see the challenge presented by this scenario, particularly in settings where there is a strong need to build up academic English, we, like Principal Lansdowne, also see the opportunity. In fact, there is much overlap between the instructional approach required to achieve advanced literacies and the pedagogical methods that best support linguistically diverse learners.

This overlap does not change the fact that today's school leaders face a "new normal" (Cordeiro & Cunningham, 2012). Preparing linguistically diverse students to communicate (orally and in writing) in diverse ways and with diverse audiences, as well as to use print for a variety of purposes, requires a different type of instruction that goes far beyond teaching basic reading and writing skills (see Chapters 2 and 3 for a discussion of *advanced literacies* and *advanced literacies leadership*). It calls for a seismic shift in the way that instruction is designed, coordinated, and delivered across classrooms in our school buildings. Beyond the strategic planning—taking the student data, teacher needs, and school conditions and characteristics into account—executing a plan that translates into differentiated instruction that supports advanced literacies for all is the ultimate challenge, demanding daily commitment and sustained attention. What makes these literacy reform efforts particularly complex is that there isn't a simple formula that can be applied at every school site. Instead, each leadership team will need to design a unique reform strategy that matches the local conditions at the site, what we refer to as a "blueprint."

Organization of This Chapter

In this chapter we support the leader, including the district leader, school-based administrators, and literacy coaches, in generating a blueprint for leading an advanced literacies reform effort—whether it's a comprehensive, mul-

---

[1] Nonmainstream dialects of English include African American English (AAE), Southern White English (SWE), and Southern African American English (SAAE) (Wolfram & Schilling-Estes, 1998).

tiyear strategy, a brief initiative to support some interim planning for deeper vocabulary instruction, or even looking to select and implement a whole new literacy curriculum. In this chapter, starting with four key distinctions that each leader must bear in mind for any instructional change effort—big or small—and a map of the advanced literacies "terrain" as we see it, we support the leader to use the tools described in Chapters 1–7, along with planning templates to generate a blueprint for moving forward. Here we attend to both the logistical issues of making these shifts at a school site, the issues related to leading and managing adults through a change process. Throughout we weave in the case example of Rosa Parks—a K–8 school with a typical middle school structure for grades 6–8. In highlighting key elements of the advanced literacies reform process at Rosa Parks School, we draw distinctions between their work in the upper elementary (grades 3–5), where one teachers serves the students in a classroom, and their work in the middle school (grades 6–8), where students rotate from classroom to classroom (and to different teachers) by content area.

Planning for Action to Promote Advanced Literacies: Four Key Distinctions to Avoid Pitfalls

To generate any action plan or blueprint in the domain of promoting advanced literacies, the leader needs to carefully understand and attend to four important distinctions, making sure that an understanding of these distinctions is reflected in the plan. Without this effort, the plan and its implementation often suffers from pitfalls that can lead to a sense of discouragement, squandered time and money, and failure to bring about improvement. As shown in Figure

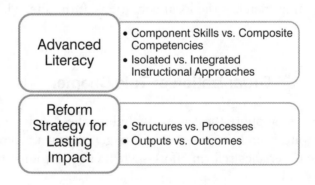

FIGURE 8.1. Four important distinctions to avoid pitfalls.

8.1, two of these distinctions are related to literacy, while the other two are about the reform strategy for lasting impact.

Literacy Distinctions

Component Skills versus Composite Competencies

In the domain of literacy, as discussed in Chapters 1 and 2, leaders must have a good handle on the distinction between *component skills* and *composite competencies* and how each supports advanced literacies learning for linguistically diverse learners and their peers. As discussed in detail in Chapter 2, *component skills* refers to very specific literacy skills (e.g., learning to match sounds to letters so as to read or spell words, or learning how to make sense of basic punctuation in a text). We can think of these skills as related to the "mechanical" aspects of reading, writing, and speaking in that they are necessary for us to read words, write words, and hear individual words in a stream of speech. They are associated with basic literacy skills, but they also support one's execution of real-world literacy tasks. *Composite competencies* are the sum or "composite" of many foundational skills working in combination with the higher-order skills. They are central to advanced literacies, whether to comprehend and synthesize sophisticated text, construct knowledge when writing, or engage in an academic debate. As our component skills develop, we are in a better position to develop composite competencies, but the latter also demand even more intensive and varied experiences interacting with text, language, and the broader world.

CASE EXAMPLE: COMPONENT SKILLS
AND COMPOSITE COMPETENCIES

Thinking back on the early years of the school's literacy reform efforts, Principal Lansdowne can still recall her early efforts to match readers with appropriate interventions. There was a time when all students who seemed to struggle with grade-level reading tasks were matched with a single intervention: a phonics program that was designed for students with persistent difficulties reading words. This tactic had done little to move most students; after all, most students weren't struggling with these basic literacies. Instead, they required more practice with the composite competencies that were needed to tackle grade-level texts, such as academic language and argumentation skills. Recognizing this fact, the current Rosa Parks model focuses less on interventions, which are not well suited for building the composite competencies that make up advanced literacies, and more on strengthening the focus on advanced literacy tasks as part of the instructional core.

Isolated versus Integrated Instructional Approaches

The other distinction leaders must grasp is that two instructional approaches together inform the design of advanced literacies teaching: the *isolated instructional approach* and the *integrated instructional approach*. In the previous chapters, we've discussed the skills and competencies that go into advanced literacies and we delineated the elements of instruction to promote those. That's the "what." But even once we're clear on the "what" with respect to skills, competencies, and instructional foci, there's the challenge of the "how." What should this instruction look and feel like? When does it make sense to focus on building up individual skills and competencies and when should we be turning to practice and inquiry in more authentic contexts? In the case of students who don't show proficiency on a specific skill or competency, when should we have them practice it in the context of an authentic task and when should we have them practice toward mastery without bringing in other demands?

The *isolated approach* is guided by the goal of augmenting a specific literacy skill or competency, and then giving learners the opportunity to hone it. This could be as narrow as practicing reading words that contain the *ea* vowel team or determining a word's meaning based on the presence of the prefix, *contra-*. Alternatively, it could be broader than that, such as working on the correct structure for writing a sentence or building fluency through repeated reading. The *integrated approach* is guided by the goal of supporting students to bring together several literacy skills and competencies simultaneously—to put multiple skills to use.[2]

ISOLATED AND INTEGRATED INSTRUCTIONAL APPROACHES	
Isolated Instructional Approach	*Integrated Instructional Approach*
The goal is to build and/or reinforce a specific skill or competency.	The goal is to support students to bring together several literacy skills and competencies simultaneously; to put multiple skills to use.

---

[2] The terms *isolated* and *integrated* instruction appear in the literature on second language teaching (see Lightbown, 1998, and Spada & Lightbown, 2008); however, we use these terms differently.

Through the instructional design process, leaders need to have this knowledge and help teachers to avoid "instructional disequilibrium," the unintended consequences that can result as they attempt to meet the call of standards-based reforms with little guidance on how to do so. For example, we've all been privy to classrooms where the individual standards are painstakingly worked on, one at a time, without ever bringing the skills together in a product or performance that reflects the real-world context. Similarly, with their focus on advanced literacy skills, the new standards may drive an overemphasis on advanced tasks and culminating projects in the absence of instruction that builds the specific literacy skills and competencies that support this type of inquiry (Bunch, Walqui, & Pearson, 2014; Davis & Wilson, 2015; Shanahan, 2014).

Developing readers require exposure to *both* isolated and integrated approaches to literacy instruction. Just think, for a moment, of a microscope in a scientist's lab. The isolated approach is akin to placing a single cell from a multicellular organism under a microscope's powerful lens. The goal of that is rarely just to understand that cell in isolation; after all, most organisms are comprised of thousands of cells! Instead, the ultimate aim of this very close-up observation is to acquire insight into how cells function within the context of a multicellular organism. But if we always start with and/or look at the multicellular organism, then we may lose important information about the way the individual parts affect the organism. Similarly, if we only look at the single cell on its own, and not in the context of the other cells, then we are likely missing important information about its functioning and purpose. Viewing instruction through the lens of these two approaches can help educators plan and implement the instruction necessary to both challenge and support diverse learners. This is not necessarily a how-to for daily lesson planning, but it is a conceptual tool to organize an overall plan for literacy instruction to ensure that the many lessons focused on specific skills and competencies are "adding up" to something that matters for advanced literacies—ensuring that students are building specific skills and competencies while also ensuring that students have opportunities to work on the kinds of projects and learning tasks that map onto real-world literacy demands.

CASE EXAMPLE: ISOLATED AND INTEGRATED
INSTRUCTIONAL APPROACHES

Teaching advanced literacies through an integrated approach had not come easily to Rosa Parks's faculty. In fact, they had stumbled at first as they tried to find their footing amid new instructional demands. Initial attempts at teaching advanced literacies in grades 6–8 (the middle school) had focused on having students write essays that drew on textual evidence. The problem was that most students were struggling to even access the text: to make sense of the academic language or to marshal the necessary background knowledge. Others had little experience with argumentation or critical interpretation. Thus, while they could summarize the text, they could not use the evidence it provided effectively. Each of these aspects would need to be addressed if students were to be successful in producing their essays. To facilitate this instruction, grade-level teams had met to break tasks into separable pieces and to co-plan instruction. These meetings often began with examining a final assignment that a teacher hoped to have students complete. Working together, the group would name the component skills and composite competencies that would support successful completion and then work to design instruction that would get students there—taking a balanced approach to the conditions under which the instruction is provided, isolated, and integrated.

Prior to the onset of Lansdowne's literacy reform initiative, a heavy focus on basic literacy skills—word reading and fluency—meant that students had little opportunity to engage in literacy instructional opportunities that took an integrated approach. And while their scores on measures of the specific skills and competencies were, in some respects, solid, it was as if the instruction failed to add up to much. The third-grade students struggled in large numbers on end-of-year state assessments. While students were encountering difficulties in the upper grades, these challenges pointed to a need to examine the "advanced literacies pipeline"; to ask challenging questions like, "How are students working on advanced literacies in isolated and integrated instructional conditions from kindergarten onward?," and, "How are these skills 'adding up' over time?" Over the course of the literacy reform effort, these questions came to inform the redesign of the instructional conditions from kindergarten to grade eight.

Strategic Reform Distinctions

Leaders must be able to take these literacy-based distinctions and consider what they mean for the strategic planning and implementation of instruction to support advanced literacies instruction (Stein & Nelson, 2005). Therefore, we turn next to key elements of the reform strategy itself. As discussed, one could in fact have deep knowledge about advanced literacies and its instruction and still not execute a successful reform effort to ensure this knowledge translates into instructional change and student gains—this is a scenario we have run into time and again. Generally it is a case of leadership not being able to avoid some common pitfalls associated with the implementation of the plan. To that end, in the domain of strategic reform for lasting impact, here we introduce two distinctions that are crucial if one is to leverage knowledge about advanced literacies to drive improvement at a site: that between a reform *structure* and a reform *process* and that between an *output* and an *outcome*.

Reform Structures versus Reform Processes

As shown in Figure 8.2, reform *structures* are the *tangible, concrete* elements of an improvement plan. In today's reform climate, such structures, as discussed in Chapters 5 and 7, might include classroom-based coaching, PLC meetings, and key tools for collecting and analyzing data. We think of these reform structures as necessary but not sufficient for lasting change. In fact, these structures could be in place—and in many schools they are—but have no net effect on the quality of teaching and learning. Why? Because the positive effects of these structures depend entirely upon the reform *processes* around them. The reform processes are the *interactions* and *continuous learning opportunities* that result from the effective use and leveraging of these structures.

CASE EXAMPLE: STRUCTURES VERSUS PROCESSES

Early in their efforts, Principal Lansdowne had set aside time each week for the middle school teachers to meet as PLCs. These structures were already

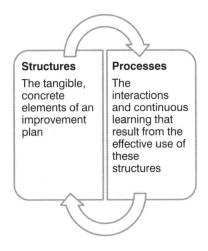

FIGURE 8.2. Reform structures and processes.

well entrenched in the elementary school, where a combination of the lack of disciplinary boundaries and the presence of common skill-building goals across classrooms made PLCs a welcome new initiative for the staff. This was not initially the case in the middle school; while teachers seemed to enjoy the chance to meet and the time was useful for discussion of students who struggled, Principal Lansdowne was disheartened that little time was actually spent focused on improving the core of instruction or troubleshooting pedagogy. Her hope had been to see PLCs support the adoption of common instructional practices (see hallmarks in Chapter 3) across classrooms, but this seemed unlikely at first given how PLCs were functioning. PLCs were a structure that the middle school needed; but devoid of knowledge of the process that PLCs typically follow, these collaborative structures were falling short. To address this issue, the leadership team clarified the purpose of these PLC meetings and supported the staff to develop protocols for examining data or looking at instruction that could turn these structures into potent contexts for instructional improvement.

Outputs versus Outcomes

The final key distinction to be made—that between *outputs* and *outcomes*—relates to how schools track and understand whether an initiative is working or not. Most often, we find that sites are confusing the two, which often makes for feelings of disappointment and frustration about the effects of an initiative. So what, exactly, is the distinction here? *Outputs* are the products of the plan's or the program's activities—they tell us that things are happening as planned. For example, individuals are participating in interventions or professional learning meetings, new curricula have been selected and implemented, and data is being analyzed and discussed in light of a new teaching–learning cycle. Administrators and staff, to cite another example, are very engaged in a specific initiative. These are all important outputs—they are indicators of the right activities proceeding as planned. *Outcomes,* on the other hand, are the changes in participants' behaviors, knowledge, and skills that we are seeking when we engage in our reform efforts and strategic planning. The outcomes as designed can and should be specific and designated short term, midterm, or long term, taking realistic expectations into account while holding tight to the notion that the change has to be at the behavioral level. It can be tempting to focus on outcomes or on outputs; it is the case, however, that every output is linked with an outcome. The inverse is also true: outcomes are inextricably linked to outputs. In schools we often face the task of mapping backward, looking at our hoped-for outcomes—changes in the way instruction is delivered and in students' advanced literacy levels—and deciding on the corresponding outputs.

Why does this distinction between outputs and outcomes matter? Having knowledge of this distinction directly addresses what we might consider to be one of the most pervasive problems tied to many strategic plans and the problem that is perhaps the most responsible for the feelings of frustration and discouragement when student scores don't show the kinds of gains that the site was expecting based on its activities and efforts. What is the problem here? Well, all too often, at a given site, the metrics for success are outputs rather than outcomes. To be sure, we won't have the desired outcomes without the outputs—but we can't stop at the outputs. If we're going to have any impact at all, then we most definitely need to have the planned activities occurring: the outputs. Without these we don't stand a chance. But we can't confuse the *outputs* with the *outcomes* that we're shooting for. We need to be able to identify both—and in our strategic planning, for every output we need a linked desired outcome. In this way, we justify the need for each activity or event by linking it to a specific outcome. In closing, we note that sites will need to use the outputs as indicators of success early in the reform process—when it wouldn't be realistic to be expecting to see growth in the desired outcomes. But even in the earliest stage of the reform, we need to be measuring the desired outcomes, to be able to capture the change over time.

CASE EXAMPLE: OUTPUTS VERSUS OUTCOMES

At the Rosa Parks School, a multiyear effort to implement a system that would link students' literacy data to program quality data is underway. In the elementary school, a data team has implemented a system. It uses an electronic spreadsheet to flag students who are encountering literacy difficulties based on screening data. These key structures are supported by a larger effort to examine the quality of daily instruction using a series of checklists to study curricula and observations to examine instruction. To date, there are many tangible outputs—a database of student- and setting-level data now exists to guide strategic planning. Meetings to discuss what the data are telling the leadership team and to design a strategic plan have taken place, and efforts to improve professional learning and to select curricula that better meet students' needs have been undertaken at the elementary school level. The outcomes are still a ways off. If their outputs lead to outcomes, perhaps in 2 years' time, the team hopes to see that students' reading scores are on the rise. Furthermore, the team hopes to see that the instruction shows more of the hallmarks of advanced literacies.

Take Action at Your Site

Taking the knowledge of what is meant by advanced literacies and of their instruction in combination with the four key distinctions highlighted above, the leader, based on our experience with our partner urban district, is equipped with the information needed to begin any literacy reform process—big or small, short term or long term.

Moving into action necessarily means a few key steps that lay the groundwork for effective, positive change. This is particularly so as it relates to ensuring that the work is prioritized and fits the conditions at the site—building off of current efforts and structures, with a clear plan. As discussed in Chapter 3, to begin any advanced literacies reform effort, irrespective of scope and depth, we strongly recommend forming a literacy team and having that team generate a mission statement, in consultation with staff. From there, based on our experience, there are several options and strategies by which to go about the work. The effectiveness of each will depend upon the other initiatives taking place at the school and the local landscape of advanced literacies instruction and its reform.

Figure 8.3 provides what we think of as the "terrain" of leading advanced literacies instruction in a linguistically diverse setting. In this culminating figure, we summarize the leadership learning, the corresponding action steps, and the concrete tools that we consider essential for moving advanced literacies work forward at a given site. We think of this map as a comprehensive resource, for which different parts would be consulted depending on what the leader and the team scope out as the work and their priorities.

From our perspective, high-impact site-based strategies are as follows:

1. *Generate a short-term plan based on an immediate need at the school site.* Engaging in the self-study process that we lay out in Chapters 4 to 7, and supported through the use of the accompanying leader's tools, literacy teams identify a key need or problem that must be acted upon immediately to support the effort toward promoting advanced literacies instruction at the site. For instance, the team might determine that without a new core curriculum or increased professional learning opportunities focused on one of the hallmarks of advanced literacies, progress is not likely. In those instances, a short-term goal may be the best course of action; this is often the case in schools that are already in the midst of a reform process, where many of the shifts described

Rethinking Literacy and Its Leadership for the 21st Century

Key Learning: Using this book as a guide, leaders can design initiatives that support 21st century advanced literacies and *also* support linguistically diverse learners.

Defining Advanced Literacies

Key Learning: Advanced literacies are composite competencies, including academic language, content/conceptual knowledge, critical interpretation, and argumentation that support students to:
1. Communicate (orally and in writing) in increasingly diverse ways and with increasingly diverse audiences.
2. Understand and use print for a variety of purposes.
3. Access and participate in academic, civic, and professional communities, where knowledge is shared and generated.

Defining Instructional Leadership for Advanced Literacies

Leadership Actions: By implementing four key shifts at the school site that address aspects of curriculum, instruction, data-to-instruction links, and professional learning, leaders can create the conditions that promote advanced literacies. Begin by inventorying the literacy landscape and by generating an advanced literacies mission statement to guide site-based reform.

Leader's Tools:
3.1 Key Shifts Inventory
3.2 Drafting an Advanced Literacies Mission Statement

Revising and Strengthening the Instructional Core

Leadership Actions:
Strengthening the instructional core requires implementing a series of high-leverage instructional practices known as the hallmarks of advanced literacies. These are:

Hallmark 1: Work with a variety of texts that feature big ideas and rich content.
Hallmark 2: Talk/discuss to build language and knowledge.
Hallmark 3: Use extended writing as a platform to build language and knowledge
Hallmark 4: Study a small set of high-utility vocabulary words needed to master language and content.
Hallmark 5: Use schoolwide protocols to support reading, writing, speaking, and listening.

Using the tool provided, examine whether the hallmarks are present in the instruction at a site.

Leader's Tool:
4.1 Instruction Inventory for the Hallmarks of Advanced Literacies

Using a Shared Curriculum or Platform to Support Daily Teaching and Learning

Leadership Action: A vertically and horizontally aligned curriculum supports advanced literacies instruction. Using the tool provided, examine the quality of curriculum currently in use or that may be adopted.

Leader's Tool:
6.1 Evaluating the Quality of Curricular Plans and Materials

Placing Data at the Core of the Literacy Improvement Effort

Leadership Action: Creating an efficient and effective assessment system addresses these key pitfalls:
1. Too much time is spent administering assessments.
2. Assessment data are not easily accessed for review and analysis.
3. There are no clear links between data gathering and instructional outcomes. Using the tools provided, inventory the assessment types in place and the time spent administering assessments at a site. Then, examine data for the purpose of strengthening the instructional core and supporting struggling readers.

Leader's Tools:
5.1 Inventory of Assessment Types and Timing
5.2 Protocol for Looking at Assessment Data

Leading the Implementation of Sustained Approaches to Staff Development

Leadership Action: Supporting advanced literacies instruction requires the redesign of adult learning at a site. Using the tool provided, examine the quality of professional learning at a site.

Leader's Tool:
7.1 Professional Learning Inventory

Bringing It All Together: Generating a Blueprint for Advanced Literacies Instruction

Leadership Action: Use the tools provided to generate short-term and long-term goals to drive advanced literacies reform.

Leader's Tools:
8.1 Selecting a Key Shift for Short-Term Action
8.2 Long-Term Goal-Setting Template
8.3 Theory-of-Change Template for Long-Term Action

A Leader's Compendium of Tools

Leader's Tools:
3.1 Key Shifts Inventory
3.2 Drafting an Advanced Literacies Mission Statement
4.1 Instruction Inventory for the Hallmarks of Advanced Literacies
5.1 Inventory of Assessment Types and Timing
5.2 Protocol for Looking at Assessment Data
6.1 Evaluating the Quality of Curricular Plans and Materials
7.1 Professional Learning Inventory
8.1 Selecting a Key Shift for Short-Term Action
8.2 Long-Term Goal-Setting Template
8.3 Theory-of-Change Template for Long-Term Action

FIGURE 8.3. A map of advanced literacy instruction in linguistically diverse settings.

in Chapter 3 have been undertaken but they lack a precursor condition (e.g., the curriculum), and/or in schools where there are too many other initiatives already underway for a sole focus on literacy at that juncture.

2. *Generate a long-term plan, limited in focus and scope: Focus on one to two priority areas.* For sites that have identified numerous priority areas via the self-study processes outlined in Chapters 3–7, a plan that first focuses on addressing one to two priorities is strongly recommended, especially because of the degree of interrelatedness across the shifts. For instance, take the case of high-quality curriculum adoption (Key Shift 3); implementing a high-quality curriculum often goes hand-in-hand with offering teachers additional professional learning opportunities (Key Shift 4) that focus on curriculum delivery, especially as it pertains to the linguistically diverse population. It is for this reason that these two shifts are often undertaken together as part of a long-term plan for literacy improvement. The focus is necessarily on getting curricular selection and implementation right. This is often the most feasible approach in schools that have already undertaken the redesign of their assessment systems (Key Shift 2) or in settings where tackling student assessment is not feasible because of district or state policies.

3. *Generate a long-term plan, comprehensive in nature: Focus on three priority areas and include a multiyear, staged plan for addressing them.* Also recognizing the nested nature of reform work, the most ambitious strategic plan for a reform process will identify multiple key shifts, and be multiyear in length. At many school sites, we have observed a similar (and logical) multiyear plan: it begins with a revision of the existing assessment and data management system (Key Shift 2), which can serve to inform the selection of a curriculum (Key Shift 1) and of instructional approaches (Key Shift 3) as well as the design of professional learning (Key Shift 4) that will meet the needs of the student population.

To support the reform leader and the members of the literacy team, we provide three different templates in the Appendix for mapping the plan and strategy:

- *Leader's Tool 8.1: Selecting a Key Shift for Short-Term Action.* This tool can be used to select a key shift as part of a short-term action plan.
- *Leader's Tool 8.2: Long-Term Goal-Setting Template.* This tool can be used to determine short-term and long-term goals that will drive reform efforts at sites.
- *Leader's Tool 8.3: Theory-of-Change Template for Long-Term Action.* At school sites where multiple shifts will be undertaken, this template pro-

REFORM IS NOT PRESCRIPTIVE

There is no prescription that can guide school reform at all sites and we encourage application of the knowledge and tools in a variety of formats and plans. Here, we are simply providing our suggestions based on our experience.

vides an organizing structure to facilitate planning. This is the most detailed planning tool we offer. It explicitly delineates the key strategic reform distinctions we discuss above.

Now, let's return to the Rosa Parks School to examine how Leader's Tool 8.3 can inform the design of literacy reform efforts at a site.

A Long-Term Plan for Literacy Reform at the Rosa Parks School: Phases 1–3

Phase 1

The literacy improvement effort at the Rosa Parks School began with assembling a standing leadership team composed of "key players" (teachers at every grade level and some who had knowledge of the needs of student subpopulations, including ELs and those who are eligible for special education). These leaders have agreed to serve on the team for 2 years to ensure that efforts are not interrupted. After drafting an advanced literacies mission statement to guide its work, the leadership team began with an examination and a redesign of its existing assessment system. First, to lead these efforts, within the literacy team, Lansdowne chose a small subgroup that would serve as the "assessment team" and be charged with creating a schoolwide database to compile the data once it had been collected (Figure 8.4). With these structures in place, the assessment team led the larger group in a self-study process during the summer before the initiative's formal roll-out, resulting in the eventual redesign of the school's assessment battery.

Like many schools, the Rosa Parks did not have screeners in place to efficiently assess students' literacy skills. After selecting two group-administered screeners that would efficiently measure key literacy skills, the team designed an assessment calendar to update the administration three times a year. A parallel effort involved the pruning of their existing battery of assessments. While formative measures (e.g., Fountas and Pinnell Benchmark Assessment), had previously been required to be administered to all elementary students

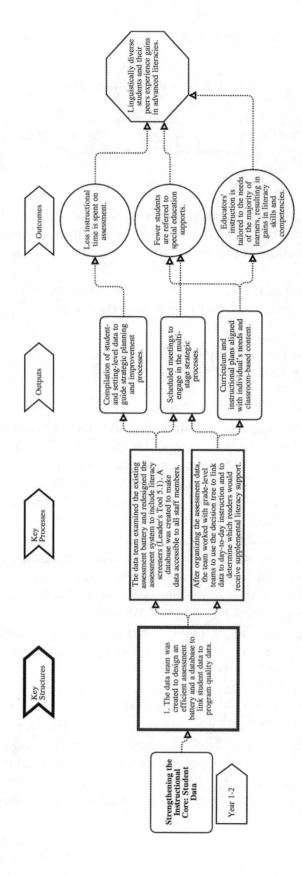

FIGURE 8.4. Creating a schoolwide database for assessment data (years 1 and 2).

at three points across the academic year, the team decided that these assessments, given their close link to instruction, should be administered by teachers as needed (see Chapter 5 for an extended discussion).

In the first year of this reform, once the screening had been administered to all students, the team celebrated its successes by looking at outputs, including (1) the compilation of student- and setting-level data that were used as part of the strategic planning process; (2) the scheduling of meetings to draft the strategic plan; and (3) the revision of the curriculum to be aligned with the needs of learners as surfaced through assessment. While it was tempting to immediately focus on outcomes—to look to see that students, including linguistically diverse learners, were demonstrating greater ability to execute advanced literacy tasks—Principal Lansdowne instead encouraged the team to focus initially on outputs; she cautioned her team that observing change in outcomes is often a longer process, and that becoming discouraged when efforts did not immediately bear fruit was a common yet avoidable misstep in the reform process. For instance, the team celebrated the launch of the schoolwide database that would be used to track student assessment data. At the same time, team members needed to be sure to begin to measure outcomes of interest and to track growth and progress (or lack thereof) toward these more distal goals.

Phase 2

In year 2 of the Rosa Parks School's advanced literacy improvement effort, the team worked to use the information on trends and patterns in students' strengths and needs surfaced through assessment data to inform the selection of a core literacy curriculum (see Figure 8.5). Focused on identifying curriculum for schoolwide adoption that would serve as a platform for instruction that exemplifies the hallmarks of advanced literacies, the team took inventory of a number of curricula (using Leader's Tool 6.1). Once a curriculum had been selected, the team designed a pilot structure for its initial implementation. In other words, a small set of "early adopters"—teachers who agreed to try it out in advance of the schoolwide initiative—implemented the curriculum, taking careful notes and completing ongoing logs and formative assessments throughout the year. Between years 2 and 3, these data were used to inform slight modifications and alterations and to promote the development of a realistic pacing plan before it was rolled out schoolwide. Again, the team celebrated outputs and recognized that outcomes would only be observed after the initial snags in the curricular implementation had been smoothed over, with the further result that new learning opportunities accumulated consis-

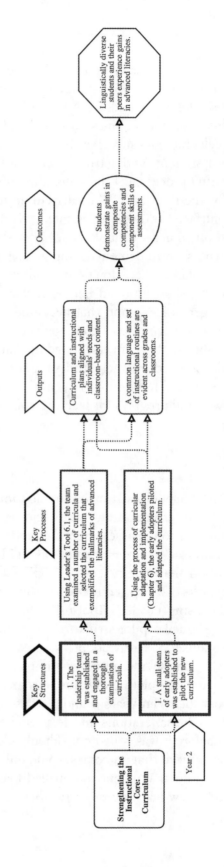

FIGURE 8.5. Using curriculum to strengthen the instructional core (year 2).

tently. It was not until the end of year 2, in fact, that the team observed that greater numbers of students were demonstrating grade-level reading ability on the end-of-year screening battery.

Phases 2 and 3

Faced with supporting educators to make sense of student data in year 1, and to translate this knowledge into practice *as well as* to support the pilot and large-scale adoption of a new curriculum in years 2 and 3, respectively, the team looked to professional learning to make their efforts a success (see Figure 8.6). Beginning in year 1 of the initiative, under the direction of Principal Lansdowne, the team put into place a series of structures to support these efforts: PLCs and a professional learning team. Using protocols and other processes to examine data, each of these constituencies set out to select professional learning priorities that responded to the needs of the learner population. With these structures and processes in place the curricular roll-out was significantly more successful than previous roll-outs had been. In this first year, professional learning focused entirely on understanding assessment and using student data to inform instruction. In year 2 onward, as the initiative ramped up, coaching was added and all professional learning was directed at creating classroom conditions that promoted advanced literacies. A key centerpiece of these efforts was the new curriculum, which was selected and adapted to meet the needs of the student population (see above); much of the professional learning opportunities centered on supporting educators to gain a level of comfort with these new materials. Certainly, these efforts did not end after a few years; instead, the staff adopted a growth mind-set in which continual iteration on instructional practices became the new normal. This was exactly what Lansdowne had hoped for. Literacy reform is a moving target and as the population at the Rosa Parks School continues to change and the science of advanced literacies instruction to evolve, so too will the instructional approach.

Taking Action: Avoiding Common Pitfalls That Impede Getting to Desired Outcomes

Laying the groundwork for an advanced literacies reform effort, including generating enthusiasm and buy-in in the form of a cross-grade and cross-content literacy team that meets regularly, and then orchestrating the development of a strategic plan, puts many school sites well ahead of the game. Many more

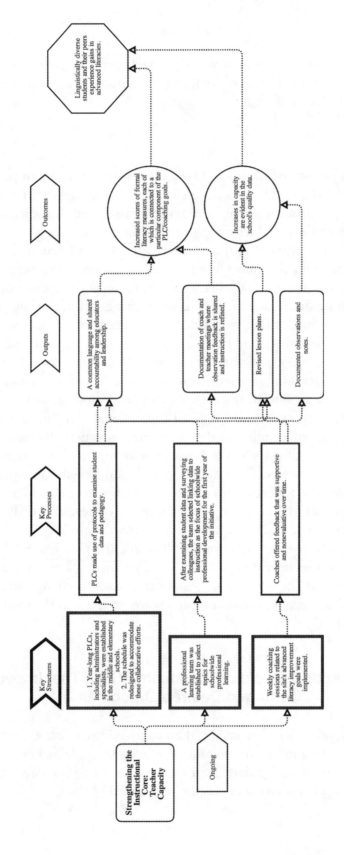

FIGURE 8.6. Putting structures in place to support professional learning (ongoing).

schools, especially those serving linguistically diverse learners, need to engage in focused, systematic, and concrete strategic planning. This kind of strategic planning results in products and guidance that is often quite different from the kinds of plans that districts and states require for accountability purposes, which often outline the "what" and "why," but not the "how."

But getting to a plan that will really drive change and ultimately the desired outcomes is not without its challenges. Over the last several years, in our work with our partner schools and district, we have identified a common set of pitfalls that plans suffer from—or at least that are overlooked during the drafting stage. These are often at the root of negligible effects or even a zero impact, giving rise to disappointment and frustration among leaders and staff who have poured valuable time and energy into the effort. As we said in Chapter 1, the problem of moving toward advanced literacies is not one of effort, but one of strategy—we're advocating for working smarter, not harder. To that end, we outline a set of three pitfalls we regularly run into, in hopes that leaders

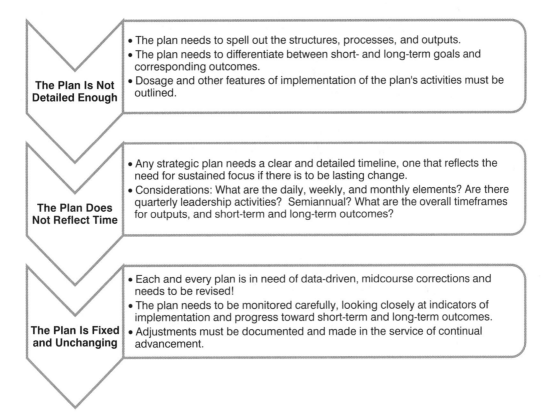

The Plan Is Not Detailed Enough
- The plan needs to spell out the structures, processes, and outputs.
- The plan needs to differentiate between short- and long-term goals and corresponding outcomes.
- Dosage and other features of implementation of the plan's activities must be outlined.

The Plan Does Not Reflect Time
- Any strategic plan needs a clear and detailed timeline, one that reflects the need for sustained focus if there is to be lasting change.
- Considerations: What are the daily, weekly, and monthly elements? Are there quarterly leadership activities? Semiannual? What are the overall timeframes for outputs, and short-term and long-term outcomes?

The Plan Is Fixed and Unchanging
- Each and every plan is in need of data-driven, midcourse corrections and needs to be revised!
- The plan needs to be monitored carefully, looking closely at indicators of implementation and progress toward short-term and long-term outcomes.
- Adjustments must be documented and made in the service of continual advancement.

FIGURE 8.7. Leading advanced literacies: Three pitfalls to avoid.

using this book and its tools as a resource to guide their work can avoid them. Summarized in Figure 8.7, these are as follows:

The Plan Is Not Detailed Enough to Drive Successful Change

• *The plan jumps from structures to desired long-term outcomes,* with no information about the processes and outputs that are needed along the way. For example, the plan might have as its desired long-term outcome to improve reading outcomes in the upper elementary grades, and might establish PLCs as a key structure for getting there, but it's missing the processes around the PLCs. What will the site do with these structures and how will the site support teachers to use them in that manner, for example—what are the outputs and short-term outcomes that link directly to the PLCs, long before we might see changes in students' reading outcomes. Not naming or identifying these processes and short-term goals, and instead simply instituting the PLCs and looking for the changes in student outcomes, is a recipe for disappointment and unnecessary feelings of failure. It also means a lack of guidance for all involved to support their implementation of the plan.

• *The plan doesn't differentiate between short- and long-term goals and corresponding outcomes.* At the classroom level, this pitfall might mean that a given plan spells out the long-term goal of improved classroom talk, but fails to articulate, for example, the short-term goals of working to promote teachers' capacity to facilitate extended discussion, meanwhile building students' capacities to use academic sentence starters and to build off of each other's comments during discussion. At the level of student skills and competencies, this pitfall might mean that a given plan is centered on improving overall reading comprehension rates but in the short term needs clearly articulated signs of progress toward that goal, such as increasing text-based discussion (output) and improving academic vocabulary (short-term goal).

• *Dosage and other features of implementation of the plan's activities are not included.* All staff who are looking to the plan to drive their daily practice need documentation that spells out the key characteristics of the activities and learning tasks (timing? format? who delivers? how often and for how long? which students? etc.) that are the core of the plan. These details are also particularly crucial for ensuring that staff turnover does not compromise or cause a setback in the reform effort. In fact, a detailed plan becomes a key tool for on-boarding new staff and ensuring that they remain for the long term.

The Plan Does Not Reflect Time

Any strategic plan needs a clear and detailed timeline—one that reflects the need for sustained focus if there is to be lasting change. Considerations: What are the daily, weekly, and monthly elements? Are there quarterly leadership activities? Semiannual? What are the overall timeframes for outputs, and for short-term and long-term outcomes?

The Plan Is Fixed and Unchanging

Getting to a detailed plan—one that is clear about implementation steps and one that reflects site-level data and input from many stakeholders—is a wonderful achievement. And then seeing that plan in action is, in some settings, an all-too-rare occurrence. It is cause for celebration, but it will lead to eventual stall-out of the effort if there is no structure and process for regularly revisiting the plan and its effects. Remember that *each and every plan will need data-driven, midcourse corrections.* The advanced literacies reform process and the document that serves as a guideline and guidepost needs to be monitored carefully by looking closely at indicators of implementation and progress toward short-term and long-term outcomes and by documenting any adjustments made in the service of continual advancement.

Conclusion

Leading Advanced Literacies Instruction

At the beginning of this book, we introduced our readers—school-based instructional leaders and those who support them—to the notion that they face new professional realities based on two key shifts in the educational landscape: (1) shifts in the school-age population and (2) shifts in the society and economy as it relates to individuals' literacy skills.

Across the nation—and this is also true for many developed countries around the world—we are educating a population that is increasingly diverse linguistically. In the United States there are over 400 native languages among the school-age population, and among these language minority learners, 20% are formally classified as ELs. By 2030, it is anticipated that 40% of the school-age population in the United States will speak a language other than English at home (Camarota, 2012). Today, in schools and districts across the United

---

A NOTE ABOUT THIS CONCLUSION

In Chapter 8, we addressed comprehensively what it takes to lead the change needed to achieve advanced literacies for all—as described in Chapters 3–7—to ensure that our students, including the growing number of linguistically diverse learners, are prepared to meet the literacy demands of today's society and economy. In this Conclusion, to close the book, we provide a very brief summary of the issues and key strategies that we outlined in the preceding chapters. The Appendix that follows provides a compendium of the leader's tools that appear throughout the book, to support advanced literacies reform in today's schools.

States, many students other than those formally classified as ELs are learning English as an additional language, even if not in the initial stages of language development. Importantly, there is an increasing number of students who speak a nonmainstream dialect of English—one that is different from the academic English of the curriculum. Thus, these students must learn the language of schooling (Washington et al., 2013).

We are educating this linguistically diverse population at the same time that what counts as "literate" is on the rise. There was a time when basic literacy skills provided a clear path forward, when extended levels of reading and writing skill were the business of higher education and only necessary for participation in white-collar professions. But today students need to develop an increasingly complex set of advanced literacy skills and competencies in order to access social and economic opportunities. Importantly, the press for advanced literacies for all does not reflect a decline in the population's literacy rates. Instead it is recognition that what counts as "literate" has changed dramatically over the last few decades (Levy & Murnane, 2005). Reading and writing have become prerequisites for participation in nearly every aspect of day-to-day, 21st-century life.

To be sure, today's context of literacy reform not only brings a challenge but also a significant opportunity. What we have spelled out in the eight previous chapters is that promoting advanced literacies for linguistically diverse students *and* meeting the demands of today's and tomorrow's standards-based reform are, in fact, compatible goals. As the reader moved through these pages, we hope it became clear that we're suggesting a focus not on *standards* per se, but on a *strong instructional design*—design that bolsters areas of weakness for linguistically diverse populations, while also focusing on their strengths as learners and individuals. In turn, the opportunity is to build upon what is already in place at a given school site, tightening the link between what is offered by way of learning experiences and opportunities and what students need—and by consequence, meeting standards and mandated initiatives as an *outcome* of these efforts.

Drawing on our partnership with one of the largest urban districts in the country and the latest research, it is clear to us that creating these instructional conditions demands enacting a series of key shifts: in the classroom curricular materials and plans; in the way data is used to inform instruction and intervention; in the nature of the instruction that students experience each day; and, finally, in how we craft professional learning for the adults in our buildings. That is the "what."

There is also the "how." To get there, school leaders have a critical role to play as patient and persistent *change agents*—the people within school sites who serve as catalysts for change by asking challenging questions and collaboratively seeking solutions to support the learner population, whether students or teachers. Being a change agent begins by identifying what needs altering at a given school site, creating the buy-in and conditions for this change, and co-constructing the work to be undertaken to get to advanced literacies for all. But actually getting there is about much more than writing up policies and plans and putting structures in place—the change agent must not only support implementation of any given plan(s) by allocating sufficient *time and resources* to the effort; he or she must also work daily to *protect the effort* by resisting other initiatives and professional activities over time.

We hope that the leader closes this book armed with the tools to identify some shortcomings of the current strategy in place—for example, asking how one's current instructional context fits the students' needs and whether the necessary conditions are in place to move toward universal advanced literacies—but definitely some potential solutions as well. You will recognize the characteristics of materials and instruction that lead to advanced literacies. You will use data to differentiate for your schools, your classrooms, and your individual students, targeting the core of instruction to the needs of the majority. You will create professional learning contexts that support teachers at your site to teach for advanced literacies development. Finally, you will undertake this work following a blueprint that can guide your efforts.

Therefore, as a final piece, the Appendix provides the reader with a compendium to support the daily work—the full set of site-evaluation and guidance tools described in the prior chapters, which together create the leader's advanced literacies toolkit. These tools should help you to both evaluate the state of current efforts and gauge progress, while also helping you to focus attention on key areas of need within the system to get to advanced literacies for all. The more we all learn about our sites, the more we can strive for continuous improvement. And while these efforts are never complete, we are incrementally closer to our goal with each line we sketch on our literacy blueprints.

APPENDIX

A Leader's Compendium of Tools

Key Shifts Inventory

Purpose: To begin to lead the key shifts at your site, first engage your team in a literacy inventory to examine the current literacy landscape: population literacy profiles, use of student assessment data, curricular and other supports for literacy, and the professional learning context.

Examining Key Shifts 1 and 2:
Who are our struggling readers and writers? How do we get this information?

Examining Key Shift 3:
What curriculum and supports do we have in place for students?

Examining Key Shift 4:
What instructional initiatives do we have in place to support literacy? What is the associated professional development?

After completing this inventory, select one key shift—your area of greatest need—to begin to tackle at your site.

(continued)

Examining Key Shifts 1 and 2: Who Are Our Struggling Readers and Writers?

- Who are our struggling readers and writers?
    - By subgroup (English-only students, reclassified English learners, English learners, etc.)?
    - Where do we get the information to classify students as struggling readers and writers (state test, teacher referrals)?
- What supports do these students receive? How do we make these decisions?

Subgroups	What percentage are struggling readers and writers?	Where do you get this information?	What supports do these students receive?

(continued)

Examining Key Shift 3: Curricular Plans and Materials to Support Literacy Teaching and Learning

- What instructional approaches and programs—daily instructional and supplemental—are in place to serve struggling literacy learners at your school?

Curriculum or intervention?	For which students?	Who designs or creates the plans and materials?	Who delivers the instructional component of this curriculum or intervention?
	☐ 3rd grade ☐ 4th grade ☐ 5th grade ☐ 6th grade ☐ 7th grade ☐ 8th grade ☐ All ☐ All ☐ ELs ☐ Special education ☐ Struggling readers	☐ Individual teachers ☐ Group of teachers ☐ District/state ☐ Prepackaged	☐ All ☐ EL specialists ☐ Bilingual teacher ☐ Reading interventionist ☐ Not teacher administered (computerized)
	☐ 3rd grade ☐ 4th grade ☐ 5th grade ☐ 6th grade ☐ 7th grade ☐ 8th grade ☐ All ☐ All ☐ ELs ☐ Special education ☐ Struggling readers	☐ Individual teachers ☐ Group of teachers ☐ District/state ☐ Prepackaged	☐ All ☐ EL specialists ☐ Bilingual teacher ☐ Reading interventionist ☐ Not teacher administered (computerized)
	☐ 3rd grade ☐ 4th grade ☐ 5th grade ☐ 6th grade ☐ 7th grade ☐ 8th grade ☐ All ☐ All ☐ ELs ☐ Special education ☐ Struggling readers	☐ Individual teachers ☐ Group of teachers ☐ District/state ☐ Prepackaged	☐ All ☐ EL specialists ☐ Bilingual teacher ☐ Reading interventionist ☐ Not teacher administered (computerized)
	☐ 3rd grade ☐ 4th grade ☐ 5th grade ☐ 6th grade ☐ 7th grade ☐ 8th grade ☐ All ☐ All ☐ ELs ☐ Special education ☐ Struggling readers	☐ Individual teachers ☐ Group of teachers ☐ District/state ☐ Prepackaged	☐ All ☐ EL specialists ☐ Bilingual teacher ☐ Reading interventionist ☐ Not teacher administered (computerized)

(continued)

Examining Key Shift 4: Instructional Initiatives (Curriculum, Interventions, or Instructional Approach) and Professional Development

- How are teachers supported in implementing these initiatives?

Initiative	Teacher supports
	☐ More than two sessions of professional learning ☐ Coaching ☐ Professional learning community (PLC) participation ☐ No professional development
	☐ More than two sessions of professional learning ☐ Coaching ☐ Professional learning community (PLC) participation ☐ One to two sessions of professional learning ☐ No professional development
	☐ More than two sessions of professional learning ☐ Coaching ☐ Professional learning community (PLC) participation ☐ One to two sessions of professional learning ☐ No professional development
	☐ More than two sessions of professional learning ☐ Coaching ☐ Professional learning community (PLC) participation ☐ One to two sessions of professional learning ☐ No professional development
	☐ More than two sessions of professional learning ☐ Coaching ☐ Professional learning community (PLC) participation ☐ One to two sessions of professional learning ☐ No professional development
	☐ More than two sessions of professional learning ☐ Coaching ☐ Professional learning community (PLC) participation ☐ One to two sessions of professional learning ☐ No professional development
	☐ More than two sessions of professional learning ☐ Coaching ☐ Professional learning community (PLC) participation ☐ One to two sessions of professional learning ☐ No professional development

Drafting an Advanced Literacies Mission Statement

Purpose: When united under a single advanced literacies mission statement—one that lays out the specific skills, competencies, and performances that we want and expect our students to demonstrate—educators are better able to create a coherent and cohesive approach to instruction. To begin drafting your mission statement, answer the questions below with your team:

- What do we believe about literacy learning and learners?
- How will we support the development of advanced literacies at our school site?

Then, use the example mission statement from the Rosa Parks School to draft your advanced literacies mission statement. This is often an ongoing process that includes refining the language with all members of the school faculty.

SAMPLE

Our mission at the Rosa Parks School is to create an advanced literacies community in which reading, writing, speaking, listening, and complex thinking are part of the everyday environment to support our students to become lifelong learners.

We believe . . .

- All students should view themselves as readers and writers as a result of participation in daily authentic reading and writing tasks and in print-rich classrooms.
- Students should be supported to communicate (orally and in writing) in increasingly diverse ways (in print, digital media) and with increasingly diverse audiences (peers, teachers, family, unfamiliar audiences, and the broader community) in each academic year.
- Students should be aided to understand and use print for a variety of purposes (to build knowledge, to be entertained, to learn about the wider world).
- All students are capable of learning to use language to learn, to think, and to communicate effectively.

—Rosa Parks School Advanced Literacies Instruction Mission Statement, Fall 2015

(continued)

Our Mission Statement:

_____

_____

_____

_____

_____

_____

_____

_____

_____

_____

_____

_____

_____

_____

_____

_____

_____

_____

_____

_____

_____

_____

_____

_____

_____

_____

_____

_____

Instructional Inventory
for the Hallmarks of Advanced Literacies

Purpose: Use this observational inventory to examine instruction for the Hallmarks.

Indicators of Hallmark 1 in Instruction	
Instructor communicates the purpose for reading the text in light of the unit's goals.	
Instructor connects the texts within the unit so that students understand the role that each text plays in building up their understanding of the unit topic.	
Instructor creates space for students to share alternative interpretations of the text.	
Instructor requires that students use text-based evidence to support any claims made about the text.	
Instructor creates opportunities for students to answer text-dependent questions through appropriately paced instruction that builds basic comprehension first, then moves to supporting readers in making inferences.	
Indicators of Hallmark 2 in Instruction	
Instructor communicates the importance of using target words when speaking.	
Instructor acknowledges the challenges associated with learning new language and conveys an attitude that values experimenting with language by praising students' attempts at using target language when speaking (i.e., an expectation that students will *not* likely use words correctly or precisely at first).	
Instructor builds in talk routines if these are not already an integral part of the curriculum.	
Students are aware of talk routines and demonstrate a level of comfort with them.	
Student discussion is part of each lesson (e.g., short peer-to-peer interaction, debates, interviews).	
Students are encouraged to use peers as language resources when speaking (e.g., to build off of others' comments, to use words first introduced by other students).	

(continued)

Indicators of Hallmark 3 in Instruction	
Instructor communicates the importance of using target words when writing.	
Instructor acknowledges the challenges associated with learning new language and conveys an attitude that values experimenting with language by acknowledging students' attempts at using target language when writing (i.e., an expectation that students will not likely use words correctly or precisely at first).	
Instructor builds in writing routines/supports if these are not already an integral part of the curriculum.	
Instructor makes students aware of the classroom's writing routines, and students demonstrate comfort with these routines.	
Instructor uses writing as a method for consolidating thinking before and after reading (e.g., summarizes or responds by sharing his or her opinion).	
Instructor encourages students to use peers and texts as language resources when writing (e.g., to use language structures and words found in mentor texts or to adopt language that peers have used successfully in their own writing or speech).	
Instructor asks students to make use of previously taught words, language structures, and strategies for academic language learning when writing.	
Indicators of Hallmark 4 in Instruction	
Instructor builds in intentional exposures to target words and features if these are not already an integral part of the curriculum.	
Instructor uses the target words when speaking and writing with the class and encourages students to do the same.	
Writing is used as a method for practicing using the target words (e.g., before and after reading; end-of-unit projects; extended essays; structured summaries).	
Indicators of Hallmark 5 in Instruction	
Instructor builds in intentional practice with schoolwide protocols.	
Instructor explains when, why, and how protocols are used. • Builds students' independent protocol use and knowledge about the learning process.	
Students show familiarity with protocols and are able to use them as a support for learning.	

Inventory of Assessment Types and Timing

Purpose: Use Part I of this inventory to identify the assessment types used at your site. Use Part II to estimate the amount of time students are presently spending participating in assessment.

Part I: Categorizing Assessment Types

Directions: Use this table as guidance for completing the grid, which is designed to support you to identify what assessments are currently in place at your site.

		Assessment Purpose	
	Characteristics	**What it can do**	**What it cannot do**
Assessment Type — **Formative**	☑ Driven by teacher observation and review of authentic reading and writing tasks	☑ Provide information on individual's overall strengths and weaknesses ☑ Identify students' instructional level ☑ Inform instructional groupings ☑ Inform lesson planning ☑ Gauge immediate learning and interest	☑ Predict future reading difficulties ☑ Compare students' performance to standards of achievement and mastery held across the country ☑ Identify profiles of risk in specific literacy subskills
Screener	☑ Quick assessment that identifies student risk for developing reading difficulties in specific literacy skills	☑ Create reader profiles that specify risks in specific literacy skills ☑ Provide a picture of greatest instructional needs across a classroom ☑ Compare students' performance to standards of achievement and mastery held across the country ☑ Predict future reading difficulties	☑ Identify the specific causes of reading difficulties or diagnostic information for intervention (i.e., signals problem but does not prescribe treatment)
Outcome	☑ Standardized tests given by state	☑ Provide information on achievement in a broad domain	☑ Inform intervention

(continued)

Inventory of Assessment Types and Timing *(page 2 of 4)*

Assessment Name	☑ Type	Notes (how determination of type was made)
	☐ Formative ☐ Screener ☐ Outcome	
	☐ Formative ☐ Screener ☐ Outcome	
	☐ Formative ☐ Screener ☐ Outcome	
	☐ Formative ☐ Screener ☐ Outcome	
	☐ Formative ☐ Screener ☐ Outcome	
	☐ Formative ☐ Screener ☐ Outcome	

(continued)

Part II: Time on Testing

Directions: For each grade level, discuss the total time spent on assessment administration as a team and record your findings in the chart below. For individually administered assessments, you will need to determine the amount of time spent administering the test to one child, then multiply it by the number of students in a class. If an assessment is given multiple times per year, you also need to multiply by the number of administration periods. For example, if a test takes 45 minutes to administer for each child, and is given three times per year, multiply 45 by the number of students in the class by 3. This will give an estimate of the amount of time it takes for one class at that grade level. If there are slight differences between two classrooms at the same grade level, based primarily on differences in the number of students, write down the middle number of hours. As a group, record how many hours are spent for each grade to create a schoolwide record. Then, compare this to the assessment time guidelines provided.

Grade:				
Assessment name	(Time to administer this assessment to an individual child) ×	(Number of children participating in individual administration in this grade) ×	(Number of times assessment is given per year) =	Total time on assessment
			Total Time	

(continued)

To evaluate your time on testing, use the guidelines below:

As schools work to implement best practices, sometimes assessment can take up too much time. As a universal battery is created, it is important to balance time on assessment with the need for instructional time. Below are our recommendations for structuring an assessment battery that efficiently screens all students in important code- and meaning-related skills, using no more than 26 hours of instructional time per year.

	Typical state requirements	**Recommended guidelines**	**Our recommended maximum**
Component-skill screening	One class period per year, with no distinction between code and meaning	Three assessments per year: September, December, and March No more than 5 hours per administration	5 hours, four times per year (20 hours total)
Composite-skill screening		Two assessment periods per year: September, February No more than 1 hour per administration	Two class periods, three times per year (6 hours total)

Protocol for Looking at Assessment Data

Purpose: This protocol is designed to facilitate data discussions in schools using a two-step process: (1) making observations about and identifying patterns in the data; and (2) generating potential explanations for and responses to patterns.

Step 1: Observations

Individual Think Time: Before beginning the discussion of the data as a group, allow all participants ample time to explore the data individually and to record their own observations.

As a Group: Share objective observations about the data.
*Avoid making conclusions, providing explanations, or drawing inferences.

For example, you might share:

Comments on quantities or proportions:

Over half of the students . . .

Over 50% of students performed below expected levels on the DIBELS; this is a 10% decrease over last year.

Note trends and patterns:

Some trends/patterns that I see are . . .

State general observations:

I observe that . . .

For Facilitators:
To help participants to keep track of ideas that have been shared, you might record major take-aways on chart paper.

Share surprise and acknowledge successes:

I'm surprised that . . .

I'm pleased that . . .

(continued)

*Based on the National School Reform Faculty.

Step 2: Explaining and Responding

Individual Think Time: Before beginning the discussion of the data as a group, allow all participants time to (1) generate potential explanations for the observed trends and patterns; (2) identify if additional data might be needed to confirm predictions; (3) propose responses related to adjustments to curriculum, professional learning, or instructional opportunities; and (4) identify data needed to monitor if the response has been effective.

As a Group: Share explanations and responses to the data using one or more of these frames:

Generate potential explanations for the observed trends and patterns (consider the role of curriculum, professional learning, or instructional opportunities):

> I believe the data suggests . . . because . . .
>
> I think that this trend may be the result of . . .

Identify additional data that might be needed to confirm predictions:

> Additional data that might confirm my explanation include . . .
>
> I would like to know more about . . .

Propose responses (consider adjustments to curriculum, professional learning, or instructional opportunities):

> Based on the data, I propose that . . .
>
> I think an appropriate response that addresses the needs I see in the data is . . .

Identify data needed to monitor if the response has been effective:

> To understand if our response has been effective, we should collect data on . . .
>
> Additional data that I think could guide implementation are . . . because . . .

Evaluating the Quality
of Curricular Plans and Materials

Purpose: Use this tool to evaluate curriculum, plans, and materials for the hallmarks.

1. The hallmarks of advanced literacies are present in all lessons and across units (see Chapter 4).	
Hallmark 1: Work with a variety of texts that feature big ideas and rich content. **Curricular Indicators**	
• Texts are closely tied to the unit. They include essential knowledge that students need to answer the "big" questions or ideas that guide the unit's assignments and learning tasks.	
• Texts tackle the unit's topics from many perspectives and angles.	
• Multiple texts of many genres or text types, including visual texts, are used throughout the unit.	
• Texts at a range of reading levels (below grade level, at grade level, above grade level) on topics that comprise the instructional focus are provided.	
• Rich, authentic literature on topics that comprise the instructional focus (books that may include vocabulary and spelling patterns that are unfamiliar to students and not be readily decodable, but offer exposure to high-level language).	
• Texts use language like that used in the discipline—the same language students need to produce during their classroom and academic work.	
• Guiding questions accompany the reading of each text (i.e., text-focused questions)—these help students to identify ideas and information central to comprehend the text.	
Hallmark 2: Talk/discuss to build language and knowledge. **Curricular Indicators**	
• Materials that support oral language activities (sentence stems for discussing texts, organizers/reproducibles to support preparation for debates) are provided.	
• Students are asked to use the target words and other academic language when speaking as part of each lesson in the unit.	

(continued)

• Speaking and listening routines (e.g., weekly debates, interviews, and other role plays) occur consistently and predictably throughout each unit. This provides students with the time and opportunity to develop mastery of these learning processes while building knowledge.	
• Students are engaged in speaking and listening as part of *each* lesson.	

Hallmark 3: Use extended writing as a platform to build language and knowledge.
Curricular Indicators

• Graphic organizers to support students in producing texts (organizers for writing narrative, how-to, and opinion texts as well as sentence stems and frames that support the writing of each text type) are provided.	
• Each lesson incorporates the need for student writing that is related to the text read or the larger topic focus.	
• The writing lessons and lesson components require students to use the unit's vocabulary words and concepts, and other academic language, when writing.	
• Writing routines (e.g., multistep processes, formats for responding to text) and tools (e.g., graphic organizers) are used consistently and predictably throughout each unit, providing students with the time and opportunity to develop mastery of these learning processes.	
• Students produce an extended writing piece as part of every unit to demonstrate their grasp of content and language (e.g., op-ed, essay, research report).	

Hallmark 4: Study a small set of high-utility vocabulary
needed to master language and content.
Curricular Indicators

• Materials for explicit teaching of vocabulary that appears in texts (student-friendly definitions, visuals, and reproducibles needed to teach words explicitly) are provided.	
• Students are exposed to target words and their features intentionally throughout the instructional cycle or unit. Multiple activities and text exposures that feature these words are intentionally built into the curriculum.	
• The words and their features (e.g., morphological characteristics) selected for teaching are essential for discussing/writing about the unit topic, and for reading the unit's multiple texts. • They are also related to other content areas and topics under study.	
• Linguistic skills that support independent word learning are in focus and taught explicitly (e.g., morphological analysis [prefix, suffix, etc.], working with context clues, parsing complex sentences).	

(continued)

Hallmark 5: Use schoolwide protocols to support reading, writing, listening, and speaking. **Curricular Indicators**	
• Each lesson or unit builds-in intentional practice with a core set of learning protocols.	
• Curriculum explains when, why and how protocols are used to build teachers' and students' skills to use protocols independently.	
2. **Tasks and texts provided in the curriculum are appropriately challenging given grade-level standards and thus support holding all students, including linguistically diverse students, to high expectations.**	
• Topics covered in the curriculum are engaging for the intended grade level.	
• Tasks and texts reflect grade-level expectations and standards.	
3. **The curricular sequence has been designed to provide ample instructional opportunities to develop target skills and competencies.**	
• Opportunities to practice newly acquired skills are prevalent.	
• Concepts and vocabulary taught appear repeatedly across a unit.	
• Skills and competencies are build incrementally.	
4. **Supports for linguistically diverse learners (and other types of learners) are explicit throughout.**	
• The content and materials relate to the cultural backgrounds of your students.	
• The curriculum provides specific adaptations for activities and the environment for students with identified disabilities or special needs.	
• The curriculum provides guidance on adaptations that can be made to meet English learners' needs.	
• The curriculum provides guidance for adapting activities and materials to support students who may speak a nonmainstream dialect of English.	
5. **To support fidelity of implementation, lesson plans provide adequate detail to execute lessons as designed and teachers are provided with all corresponding materials.**	
• A required or suggested structure and schedule for instruction and activities is provided.	
• A detailed instructional guide, including sample lesson plans, is provided.	
• All materials required for instruction are included.	
• Authentic supplementary materials are provided to extend instruction.	

(continued)

• Formative assessments are embedded within the curriculum and guidelines are given to teachers to understand progress and development of skills and competencies.	
6. The curriculum serves an educative function by providing teachers a rationale for the design of each activity and task.	
• Teacher tips and explanations for the design of curricular activities are prevalent throughout the curriculum.	
• There is a front-matter section that explains the design of the curriculum.	

Professional Learning Inventory

Purpose: Use this tool to evaluate whether your professional learning environment supports advanced literacies instruction.

Professional Development: Format

Educator Participation	
• At each session, educators openly share thoughts, discuss perspectives, and raise questions (even when the question may reflect a lack of understanding).	
• At each session, participants acquire new knowledge, reflect on the ideas with colleagues, and give feedback.	
• Our PD sessions can be characterized as highly interactive and engaging.	
Structures to Support Application to Everyday Practice	
• Materials necessary for implementing new knowledge are available and accessible.	
• Formal collaboration time among educators is regular and frequent (via PLCs or coaching). ▪ Designated opportunities for educators to share newly acquired knowledge.	
• Nonevaluative observations and feedback are ongoing (via PLCs or coaching).	
• Schedules and classroom locations are organized to best encourage informal discussions about instruction.	

Professional Development: Substance

Site-Level Needs	
• Our PD effort is part of a long-term improvement plan guided by **patterns in student data.**	
• Our PD effort is part of a long-term improvement plan guided by **staff professional needs.**	
• Our PD effort is part of a long-term improvement plan guided by **organizational goals.**	
• Our PD effort is explicitly **connected to the curriculum.**	

(continued)

Intensive and Continuous Support for Educators	
• Our PD opportunities **build off of each other** to encourage in-depth learning.	
• Our PD plan includes **ongoing training embedded in daily practice.**	
• Our PD plan integrates high-level theory and rationales (**i.e., *why, what***) with practice-based activities (**i.e., *how***), using case studies, data analyses, demonstrations, lesson designs, etc.	
• **Post-PD supports** (e.g., materials, learning communities) are part of the plan.	

Selecting a Key Shift for Short-Term Action

Purpose: You will work with your school-based colleagues to determine which shift you will design an implementation plan around, as part of the overall reform strategy at your site. Bear in mind that each shift is intentionally broad, encompassing many aspects of literacy reform—within each, schools may face any number of pressing challenges. For example:

Shift 1	Shift 2	Shift 3	Shift 4
• From supporting diverse learners through interventions . . . To focusing on the instructional core.	• From using data on the edges of our efforts . . . To placing data at the core of the literacy improvement effort.	• From having practitioners design and deliver instruction . . . To using a shared curriculum to support daily teaching and learning.	• From using one-size-fits-all professional development . . . To creating 21st-century adult learning environments.
Sample Pressing Problems:	**Sample Pressing Problems:**	**Sample Pressing Problems:**	**Sample Pressing Problems:**
• We lack a set of core instructional practices that take place in all classrooms (e.g., accountable talk, questioning the author, CSR). • We lack a common language for discussing instructional goals and practices. • We have not had a PD effort to support grade-level teams to determine and implement hallmarks of advanced literacy practices in all classrooms.	• We lack the data to ensure a strategic match between the readers' individual needs. • We are unclear on the skills our specific interventions address. • We are unsure if our interventions are implemented with fidelity; we lack ongoing data on implementation. • We struggle to link data to daily instructional plans for all.	• We lack a core curriculum. • We must strategically and systematcially adapt our core curriculum to meet our students' needs. • Our staff is unfamiliar with (and lacks confidence to implement) the aspects of our core curriculum that support advanced literacy. • We have had minimal PD focused on our instructional materials. • Our implementation is inconsistent and lacks a guiding plan.	• We have had little PD to build knowledge about literacy instruction for ELs. • Our PLCs need stronger emphasis on and support for building knowledge of advanced literacy. • Scheduling must be addressed to make a sustained approach possible. • We lack a professional development plan that is cohesive; and/or someone to lead this initiative.

(continued)

Step 1: Identifying Your Key Shift and Pressing Problem

Examine your inventories as a school team to determine your key shift for literacy reform. Select the shift that is the highest priority (i.e., would have the highest impact) for your school site at this time, in light of the students and the educators. Then, identify a single pressing problem to address within your shift (see previous examples).

Step 2: Goal Setting

After selecting your pressing problem, select a short-term goal (i.e., for this school year) and a long-term goal (i.e., for the next school year). A short-term goal should be accomplished within one academic year; a long-term goal may require additional steps to achieve and may only be accomplished with a longer timeline.

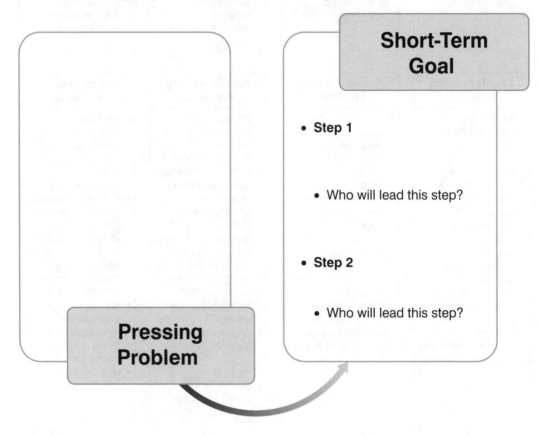

Pressing Problem

Short-Term Goal

- **Step 1**

  - Who will lead this step?

- **Step 2**

  - Who will lead this step?

Long-Term Goal-Setting Template

Purpose: You will work with your school-based colleagues to determine which shift you will design an implementation plan around, as part of the overall reform strategy at your site. Bear in mind that each shift is intentionally broad, encompassing many aspects of literacy reform—within each, schools may face any number of pressing challenges. For example:

Shift 1	Shift 2	Shift 3	Shift 4
• From supporting diverse learners through interventions . . . To focusing on the instructional core.	• From using data on the edges of our efforts . . . To placing data at the core of the literacy improvement effort.	• From having practitioners design and deliver instruction . . . To using a shared curriculum to support daily teaching and learning.	• From using one-size-fits-all professional development . . . To creating 21st-century adult learning environments.

Sample Pressing Problems:	Sample Pressing Problems:	Sample Pressing Problems:	Sample Pressing Problems:
• We lack a set of core instructional practices that take place in all classrooms (e.g., accountable talk, questioning the author, CSR). • We lack a common language for discussing instructional goals and practices. • We have not had a PD effort to support grade-level teams to determine and implement hallmarks of advanced literacy practices in all classrooms.	• We lack the data to ensure a strategic match between the readers' individual needs. • We are unclear on the skills our specific interventions address. • We are unsure if our interventions are implemented with fidelity; we lack ongoing data on implementation. • We struggle to link data to daily instructional plans for all.	• We lack a core curriculum. • We must strategically and systematcially adapt our core curriculum to meet our students' needs. • Our staff is unfamiliar with (and lacks confidence to implement) the aspects of our core curriculum that support advanced literacy. • We have had minimal PD focused on our instructional materials. • Our implementation is inconsistent and lacks a guiding plan.	• We have had little PD to build knowledge about literacy instruction for ELs. • Our PLCs need stronger emphasis on and support for building knowledge of advanced literacy. • Scheduling must be addressed to make a sustained approach possible. • We lack a professional development plan that is cohesive; and/or someone to lead this initiative.

(continued)

Step 1: Identifying Your Shift and Pressing Problem

Examine your inventories as a school team to determine your shift for literacy reform. Select the shift that is the highest priority (i.e., would have the highest impact) for your school site at this time, in light of the students and the educators. Then, identify a single pressing problem to address within your shift (see examples above).

Step 2: Goal Setting

After selecting your pressing problem, select a short-term goal (i.e., for this school year) and a long-term goal (i.e., for the next school year). A short-term goal should be accomplished within one academic year; a long-term goal may require additional steps to achieve and may only be accomplished with a longer timeline.

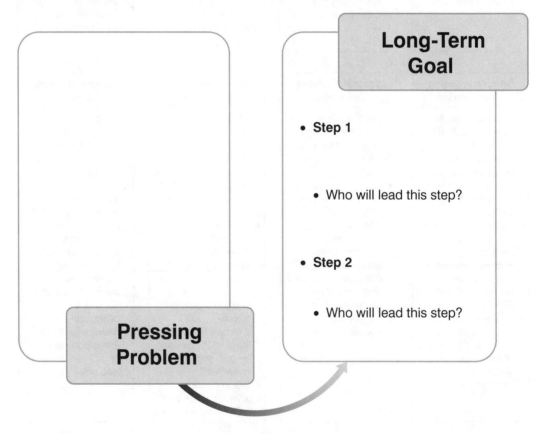

Long-Term Goal

- **Step 1**

  - Who will lead this step?

- **Step 2**

  - Who will lead this step?

Pressing Problem

(continued)

Long-Term Goal-Setting Template *(page 3 of 3)*

Step 3: What Action Steps Will You Take?

Having selected a specific shift, determine with your team the first two action steps that you will take to address your goals.

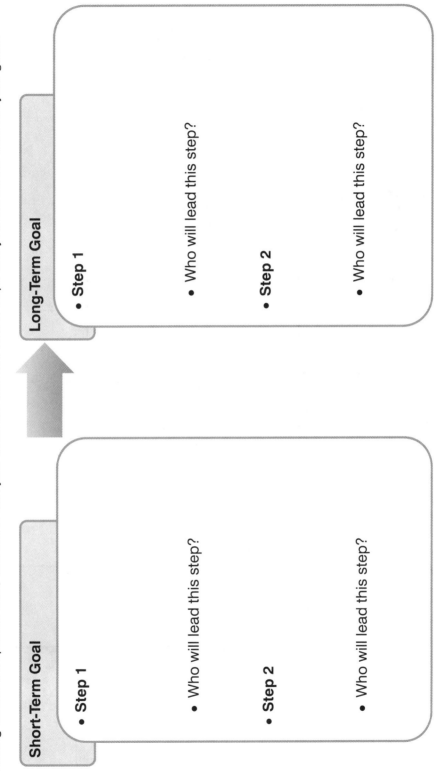

Short-Term Goal

- **Step 1**
  - Who will lead this step?
- **Step 2**
  - Who will lead this step?

Long-Term Goal

- **Step 1**
  - Who will lead this step?
- **Step 2**
  - Who will lead this step?

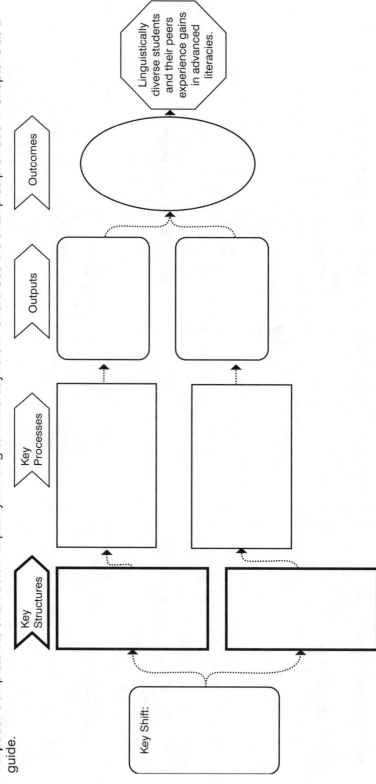

Theory-of-Change Template for Long-Term Action

Purpose: Complete the chart below to plan your long-term literacy reform effort. Use the examples provided in Chapter 8 as a guide.

Outcomes

Outputs

Key Processes

Key Structures

Linguistically diverse students and their peers experience gains in advanced literacies.

Key Shift:

References

Al Otaiba, S., & Fuchs, D. (2002). Characteristics of children who are unresponsive to early literacy intervention: A review of the literature. *Remedial and Special Education, 23*(5), 300–316.

Anmarkrud, Ø., Bråten, I., & Strømsø, H. I. (2014). Multiple-documents literacy: Strategic processing, source awareness, and argumentation when reading multiple conflicting documents. *Learning and Individual Differences, 30,* 64–76.

Arya, D. J., Hiebert, E. H., & Pearson, P. D. (2011). The effects of syntactic and lexical complexity on the comprehension of elementary science texts. *International Electronic Journal of Elementary Education, 4*(1), 107–125.

Aud, S., Hussar, W., Kena, G., Bianco, K., Frohlich, L., Kemp, J., et al. (2011). *The condition of education 2011* (U.S. Department of Education, National Center for Education Statistics; NCES 2011-033). Washington, DC: U.S. Government Printing Office.

August, D., McCardle, P., & Shanahan, T. (2014). Developing literacy in English language learners: Findings from a review of the experimental research. *School Psychology Review, 43*(4), 490–498.

August, D., & Shanahan, T. (2006). *Executive summary: Developing literacy in second-language learners: Report of the National Literacy Panel on Language-Minority Children and Youth.* Mahwah, NJ: Erlbaum.

Aukerman, M. (2013). Rereading comprehension pedagogies: Toward a dialogic teaching ethic that honors student sensemaking. *Dialogic Pedagogy: An International Online Journal, 1,* A1–A31.

Baker, L., Dreher, M. J., Shiplet, A. K., Beall, L. C., Voelker, A. N., Garrett, A. J., et al. (2011). Children's comprehension of informational text: Reading, engaging, and learning. *International Electronic Journal of Elementary Education, 4*(1), 197–227.

Barzilai, S., & Eshet-Alkalai, Y. (2015). The role of epistemic perspectives in comprehension of multiple author viewpoints. *Learning and Instruction, 36,* 86–103.

Beck, I. L., McKeown, M. G., & Kucan, L. (2013). *Bringing words to life: Robust vocabulary instruction* (2nd ed.). New York: Guilford Press.

Bhattacharya, A. (2010). Children and adolescents from poverty and reading development: A research review. *Reading and Writing Quarterly, 26*(2), 115–139.

Bialystok, E., Craik, F. I. M., & Luk, G. (2012). Bilingualism: Consequences for mind and brain. *Trends in Cognitive Science, 16*(4), 240–250.

Blachowicz, C., Ogle, D., Fisher, P., & Taffe, S. W. (2013). *Teaching academic vocabulary K–8: Effective practices across the curriculum.* New York: Guilford Press.

Boudett, K. P., City, E., & Murnane, R. (Eds.). (2005). *Data wise: A step-by-step guide to using assessment results to improve teaching and learning.* Cambridge, MA: Harvard Education Press.

Britton, B. K., & Graesser, A. C. (Eds.). (2014). *Models of understanding text.* New York: Psychology Press.

Brown, J. E., & Doolittle, J. (2008, May–June). A cultural, linguistic, and ecological framework for response to intervention with English language learners. *Teaching Exceptional Children, 40*(5), 66–72.

Bunch, G. C., Walqui, A., & Pearson, P. D. (2014). Complex text and new common standards in the United States: Pedagogical implications for English learners. *TESOL Quarterly, 48*(3), 533–559.

Camarota, S. (2012). *Immigrants in the United States: A profile of America's foreign-born population.* Washington, DC: Center for Immigration Studies.

Carlisle, J. F. (2000). Awareness of the structure and meaning of morphologically complex words: Impact on reading. *Reading and Writing, 12*(3), 169–190.

Christ, T. J., Monaghen, B. D., Zopluoglu, C., & Van Norman, E. R. (2013). Curriculum-based measurement of oral reading evaluation of growth estimates derived with pre–post assessment methods. *Assessment for Effective Intervention, 38*(3), 139–153.

Christ, T. J., Zopluoglu, C., Monaghen, B. D., & Van Norman, E. R. (2013). Curriculum-based measurement of oral reading: Multi-study evaluation of schedule, duration, and dataset quality on progress monitoring outcomes. *Journal of School Psychology, 51*(1), 19–57.

Coleman, R., & Goldenberg, C. (2012). The Common Core challenge for ELLs. *Principal Leadership, 12*(5), 46–51.

Compton, D. L., Miller, A. C., Elleman, A. M., & Steacy, L. M. (2014). Have we forsaken reading theory in the name of "quick fix" interventions for children with reading disability? *Scientific Studies of Reading, 18*(1), 55–73.

Cordeiro, P. A., & Cunningham, W. G. (2012). *Educational leadership: A bridge to improved practice* (5th ed.). Old Tappan, NJ: Pearson Higher Education.

Cummings, K. D., Biancarosa, G., Schaper, A., & Reed, D. K. (2014). Examiner error in curriculum-based measurement of oral reading. *Journal of School Psychology, 52*(4), 361–375.

Daly, E. J., Neugebauer, S., Chafouleas, S., & Skinner, C. H. (2015). *Interventions for reading problems: Designing and evaluating effective strategies.* New York: Guilford Press.

Darling-Hammond, L., Wei, R. C., Andree, A., Richardson, N., & Orphanos, S. (2009). *Professional learning in the learning profession.* Washington, DC: National Staff Development Council.

Davis, D. S., & Wilson, A. (2015). Practices and commitments of test-centric literacy instruction: Lessons from a testing transition. *Reading Research Quarterly, 50*(3), 357–359.

Davis, E. A., & Krajcik, J. S. (2005). Designing educative curriculum materials to promote teacher learning. *Educational Researcher, 34*(3), 3–14.

Deacon, S. H., & Kirby, J. R. (2004). Morphological awareness: Just "more phonological"?: The roles of morphological and phonological awareness in reading development. *Applied Psycholinguistics, 25*(02), 223–238.

de Jong, E. J., & Harper, C. A. (2004). Is ESL just good teaching? In *Proceedings of the Third International Conference on Language Teacher Education* (CARLA Working Paper No. 24). Minneapolis, MN: University of Minnesota, Center for Advanced Research on Language Acquisition. Retrieved from *www.carla.umn.edu/resources/working-papers*.

Desimone, L. M., Porter, A. C., Garet, M. S., Yoon, K. S., & Birman, B. F. (2002). Effects of professional development on teachers' instruction: Results from a three-year longitudinal study. *Educational Evaluation and Policy Analysis, 24*(2), 81–112.

Elmore, R. (2008). Leadership as the practice of improvement. *Improving School Leadership, 2*, 37–67.

Fischer, K. W., & Pruyne, E. (2003). Reflective thinking in adulthood. In J. Demick & C. Andreoletti (Eds.), *Handbook of adult development* (pp. 169–198). New York: Springer.

Francis, D. J., Rivera, M., Lesaux, N. K., Kieffer, M. J., & Rivera, H. (2006, October). *Practical guidelines for the education of English language learners.* Presentation at LEP Partnership Meeting. Washington, DC. Available at *www.centeroninstruction.org*.

Garcia, E., & Cuéllar, D. (2006). Who are these linguistically and culturally diverse students? *Teachers College Record, 108*(11), 2220–2246.

Genesee, F., Geva, E., Dressler, C., & Kamil, M. (2006). Synthesis: Cross-linguistic relationships. In D. August & T. Shananan (Eds.), *Developing literacy in second-language learners: Report of the National Literacy Panel on Language-Minority Children and Youth* (pp. 153–174). Mahwah, NJ: Erlbaum.

Gersten, R., & Baker, S. (2000). What we know about effective instructional practices for English-language learners. *Exceptional Children, 66*(4), 454–470.

Geva, E., & Yaghoub Zadeh, Z. (2006). Reading efficiency in native English-speaking and English-as-a-second-language children: The role of oral proficiency and underlying cognitive–linguistic processes. *Scientific Studies of Reading, 10*(1), 31–57.

Goodman, K. S. (2006). *The truth about DIBELS: What it is, what it does.* Portsmouth, NH: Heinemann.

Goodwin, A. P., Huggins, A. C., Carlo, M. S., August, D., & Calderon, M. (2013). Minding morphology: How morphological awareness relates to reading for English language learners. *Reading and Writing, 26*(9), 1387–1415.

Graham, S., Early, J., & Wilcox, K. (2014). Adolescent writing and writing instruction: Introduction to the special issue. *Reading and Writing, 27*(6), 969–972.

Graham, S., & Perin, D. (2007). *Writing next: Effective strategies to improve writing of adolescents in middle and high schools. A Report to the Carnegie Corporation of New York.* Washington, DC: Alliance for Excellent Education.

Graves, M. F., Baumann, J. F., Blachowicz, C. L., Manyak, P., Bates, A., Cieply, C., et al. (2014). Words, words everywhere, but which ones do we teach? *The Reading Teacher, 67*(5), 333–346.

Gravois, T. A., & Rosenfield, S. A. (2006). Impact of instructional consultation teams on the disproportionate referral and placement of minority students in special education. *Remedial and Special Education, 27*(1), 42–52.

Grosjean, F. (1998). Studying bilinguals: Methodological and conceptual issues. *Bilingualism: Language and Cognition, 1*, 131–149.

Guthrie, J. T., Wigfield, A., & You, W. (2012). Instructional contexts for engagement and achievement in reading. In S. L. Christenson, A. L. Reschly, & C. Wylie (Eds.), *Handbook of research on student engagement* (pp. 601–634). New York: Springer.

Harry, B., & Klingner, J. (2014). *Why are so many minority students in special education?* New York: Teachers College Press.

Heath, S. B. (2012). *Words at work and play: Three decades in family and community life.* New York: Cambridge University Press.

Heritage, M., Walqui, A., & Linquanti, R. (2015). *English language learners and the new standards: Developing language, content knowledge, and analytical practices in the classroom.* Cambridge, MA: Harvard Education Press.

Hiebert, E. H. (2013). Supporting students' movement up the staircase of text complexity. *The Reading Teacher, 66*(6), 459–468.

Hirsch, E. D. Jr., & Hansel, L. (2013). Why content is king. *Educational Leadership, 71*(3), 28–33.

Huizinga, T., Handelzalts, A., Nieveen, N., & Voogt, J. M. (2014). Teacher involvement in curriculum design: Need for support to enhance teachers' design expertise. *Journal of Curriculum Studies, 46*(1), 33–57.

Huizinga, T., Handelzalts, A., Nieveen, N., & Voogt, J. M. (2015). Fostering teachers' design expertise in teacher design teams: Conducive design and support activities. *Curriculum Journal, 26*(1), 137–163.

Hull, G. A., & Moje, E. B. (2012). What is the development of literacy the development of? In K. Hakuta & M. Santos (Eds.), *Understanding language: Commissioned papers on language and literacy issues in the Common Core State Standards and Next Generation Science Standards* (pp. 64–74). Stanford, CA: Stanford University.

Janssen, J., Kirschner, F., Erkens, G., Kirschner, P. A., & Paas, F. (2010). Making the black box of collaborative learning transparent: Combining process-oriented and cognitive load approaches. *Educational Psychology Review, 22*(2), 139–154.

Joyce, B. R., & Showers, B. (2002). *Student achievement through staff development.* Alexandria, VA: ASCD.

Kieffer, M. J. (2008). Catching up or falling behind?: Initial English proficiency, concentrated poverty, and the reading growth of language minority learners in the United States. *Journal of Educational Psychology, 100*(4), 851–868.

Kieffer, M. J., Biancarosa, G., & Mancilla-Martinez, J. (2013). Roles of morphological awareness in the reading comprehension of Spanish-speaking language minority learners: Exploring partial mediation by vocabulary and reading fluency. *Applied Psycholinguistics, 34*(04), 697–725.

Kieffer, M. J., & Vukovic, R. K. (2012). Components and context: Exploring sources of reading difficulties for language minority learners and native English speakers in urban schools. *Journal of Learning Disabilities, 45*(5), 433–452.

Klingner, J., & Eppolito, A. (2014). *English language learners: Differentiating between language acquisition and learning disabilities.* Arlington, VA: Council for Exceptional Children.

Kovaleski, J. F., & Pederson, J. (2008). Best practices in data analysis teaming. In A. Thomas & J. Grimes (Eds.), *Best practices in school psychology V* (pp. 115–130). Bethesda, MD: National Association of School Psychologists.

Lawrence, J. F., Phillips Galloway, E., Yim, S., & Lin, A. (2013). Learning to write in middle school? *Journal of Adolescent and Adult Literacy, 57*(2), 151–161.

Lemke, J. L. (1990). *Talking science: Language, learning, and values.* Norwood, NJ: Ablex.

Lesaux, N. K., Harris, J. R., & Sloane, P. (2012). Adolescents' motivation in the context of an academic vocabulary intervention in urban middle school classrooms. *Journal of Adolescent and Adult Literacy, 56*(3), 231–240.

Lesaux, N. K., & Kieffer, M. J. (2010). Exploring sources of reading comprehension difficulties among language minority learners and their classmates in early adolescence. *American Educational Research Journal, 47*(3), 596–632.

Lesaux, N. K., Kieffer, M. J., Faller, S. E., & Kelley, J. G. (2010). The effectiveness and ease of implementation of an academic vocabulary intervention for linguistically diverse students in urban middle schools. *Reading Research Quarterly, 45*(2), 196–228.

Lesaux, N. K., Kieffer, M. J., Kelley, J. G., & Harris, J. R. (2014). Effects of academic vocabulary instruction for linguistically diverse adolescents: Evidence from a randomized field trial. *American Educational Research Journal, 51*(6), 1159–1194.

Lesaux, N. K., Lipka, O., & Siegel, L. S. (2006). Investigating cognitive and linguistic abilities that influence the reading comprehension skills of children from diverse linguistic backgrounds. *Reading and Writing, 19*(1), 99–131.

Lesaux, N. K., & Marietta, S. H. (2011). *Making assessment matter: Using test results to differentiate reading instruction.* New York: Guilford Press.

Lesaux, N. K., Rupp, A. A., & Siegel, L. S. (2007). Growth in reading skills of children from diverse linguistic backgrounds: Findings from a 5–year longitudinal study. *Journal of Educational Psychology, 99*(4), 821–834.

Lesaux, N. K., & Siegel, L. S. (2003). The development of reading in children who speak English as a second language. *Developmental Psychology, 39*(6), 1005–1019.

Levy, F., & Murnane, R. (2005). *How computerized work and globalization shape human skill demands* (Massachusetts Institute of Technology IPC Working Paper Series). Cambridge, MA: MIT.

Lewis, C. C. (2002). *Lesson study: A handbook of teacher-led instructional change.* Philadelphia: Research for Better Schools.

Louis, K. S., Leithwood, K., Wahlstrom, K. L., & Anderson, S. E. (2010). *Learning from leadership: Investigating the links to improved student learning* (Final Report on Research to the Wallace Foundation). St. Paul, MN: Center for Applied Research and Educational Improvement, University of Minnesota.

Lucas, T., Villegas, A. M., & Freedson-Gonzalez, M. (2008). Linguistically responsive teacher education preparing classroom teachers to teach English language learners. *Journal of Teacher Education, 59*(4), 361–373.

Mancilla-Martinez, J., & Lesaux, N. K. (2011). Predictors of reading comprehension for struggling readers: The case of Spanish-speaking language minority learners. *Journal of Educational Psychology, 102*(3), 701–711.

McDonald, J. P., Mohr, N., Dichter, A., & McDonald, E. C. (2014). *The power of protocols.* New York: Teachers College Press.

Michaels, S., O'Connor, M. C., Hall, M. W., & Resnick, L. (2002). *Accountable talk: Classroom conversation that works.* Pittsburgh, PA: University of Pittsburgh.

Moats, L. C. (2000). *Speech to print: Language essentials for teachers.* Baltimore, MD: Brookes.

Moje, E. B. (2007). Developing socially just subject-matter instruction: A review of the literature on disciplinary literacy teaching. *Review of Research in Education, 31*(1), 1–44.

Murnane, R. J., Sharkey, N. S., & Boudett, K. P. (2005). Using student-assessment results to improve instruction: Lessons from a workshop. *Journal of Education for Students Placed at Risk, 10*(3), 269–280.

Murphy, P. K., Rowe, M. L., Ramani, G., & Silverman, R. (2014). Promoting critical-analytic thinking in children and adolescents at home and in school. *Educational Psychology Review, 26*(4), 561–578.

Murphy, P. K., Wilkinson, I. A., Soter, A. O., Hennessey, M. N., & Alexander, J. F. (2009). Examining the effects of classroom discussion on students' comprehension of text: A meta-analysis. *Journal of Educational Psychology, 101*(3), 740–764.

Nagy, W., Berninger, V. W., & Abbott, R. D. (2006). Contributions of morphology beyond phonology to literacy outcomes of upper elementary and middle-school students. *Journal of Educational Psychology, 98*(1), 134–147.

Nagy, W., & Townsend, D. (2012). Words as tools: Learning academic vocabulary as language acquisition. *Reading Research Quarterly, 47*(1), 91–108.

National Center for Education Statistics. (2009). *Table A-6–1. Number and percentage distribution of 3- to 21-year olds served under the Individuals with Disabilities Act (IDEA), Part B, and number served as a percentage of total public school enrollment, by type of disability: Selected school years, 1976–1977 through 2007–2008.* Washington, DC: Institute of Education Sciences, U.S. Department of Education.

Nelson, J., Benner, G. J., & Gonzalez, J. (2003). Learner characteristics that influence the treatment effectiveness of early literacy interventions: A meta-analytic review. *Learning Disabilities Research and Practice, 18*(4), 255–267.

Norris, S., Phillips, L., & Osborne, J. (2006). Scientific inquiry: The place of interpretation and argumentation. In J. Luft, R. L. Bell, & J. Gess-Newsome (Eds.), *Science as inquiry in the secondary setting* (pp. 87–98). Arlington, VA: NSTA Press.

Organization for Economic Cooperation and Development. (2010). *PISA 2009 results: Overcoming social background—Equity in learning opportunities and outcomes* (Vol. 2). Paris: Author.

Orosco, M., & Klinger, J. K. (2010). One school's implementation of RTI with English language learners: "Referring into RTI." *Journal of Learning Disabilities, 43*, 269–288.

Ortiz, A., & Artiles, A. J. (2010). Meeting the needs of ELLs with disabilities: A linguistically and culturally responsive model. In G. Li & P. A. Edwards (Eds.), *Best practices in ELL instruction* (pp. 247–272). New York: Guilford Press.

Pacheco, M. B., & Goodwin, A. P. (2013). Putting two and two together: Middle school students' morphological problem: Solving strategies for unknown words. *Journal of Adolescent and Adult Literacy, 56*(7), 541–553.

Paine, S. (2004). Supporting a school-wide reading initiative by working with curriculum, instruction, and assessment variables. Available at *http://reading.uoregon.edu/resources/downloads/ldrship_CIA.pdf.*

Palinscar, A. S., & Brown, A. L. (1984). Reciprocal teaching of comprehension-fostering and comprehension-monitoring activities. *Cognition and Instruction, 1*(2), 117–175.

Peery, A. B. (2004). *Deep change: Professional development from the inside out.* Oxford, UK: Scarecrow Education.

Peña, E. D., Bedore, L. M., & Gillam, R. B. (2011). Two to untangle: Language impairment and language differences in bilinguals. *AccELLerate!: The Quarterly Review of the National Clearinghouse for English Language Acquisition, 3*(3), 7–9.

Phillips Galloway, E., & Lesaux, N. (2015). Reading comprehension skill development and instruction for adolescent English language learners: A focus on academic vocabulary instruction. In K. L. Santi & D. K. Reed (Eds.), *Improving reading comprehension of middle and high school students* (pp. 153–178). New York: Springer.

Phillips Galloway, E., Stude, J., & Uccelli, P. (2015). Students' reflections on academic language. *Linguistics and Education, 31,* 221—237.

Pressley, M., & Afflerbach, P. (1995). *Verbal protocols of reading: The nature of constructively responsive reading.* Hillsdale, NJ: Erlbaum.

Qian, G., & Alvermann, D. E. (2000). Relationship between epistemological beliefs and conceptual change learning. *Reading and Writing Quarterly, 16*(1), 59–74.

Rodriguez, D., Carrasquillo, A., & Lee, K. S. (2014). *The bilingual advantage: Promoting academic development, biliteracy, and native language in the classroom.* New York: Teachers College Press.

Ryan, J. (2010). *Five miles away, a world apart: One city, two schools, and the story of educational opportunity in modern America.* Oxford, UK: Oxford University Press.

Samway, K. D., & McKeon, D. (Eds.). (2007). *Myths and realities: Best practices for English language learners* (2nd ed.). Portsmouth, NH: Heinemann.

Scarcella, R. (2003). *Academic English: A conceptual framework* (Technical Report 2003-1). Irvine, CA: University of California Linguistic Minority Research Institute.

Schleppegrell, M. J. (2004). *The language of schooling: A functional linguistics perspective.* Mahwah, NJ: Erlbaum.

Selman, R. L. (2003). *The promotion of social awareness: Powerful lessons for the partnership of developmental theory and classroom practice.* New York: Russell Sage Foundation.

Shanahan, T. (2014). Educational policy and literacy instruction. *The Reading Teacher, 68*(1), 7–12.

Shapiro, E. S., Zigmond, N., Wallace, T., & Marston, D. (Eds.). (2011). *Models for implementing response to intervention: Tools, outcomes, and implications.* New York: Guilford Press.

Short, D. J., & Fitzsimmons, S. (2007). *Double the work: Challenges and solutions to acquiring language and academic literacy for adolescent English language learners. A report to Carnegie Corporation of New York.* Washington, DC: Alliance for Excellent Education.

Snow, C. E. (2010). Academic language and the challenge of reading for learning about science. *Science, 328*(5977), 450–452.

Snow, C. E., & Uccelli, P. (2009). The challenge of academic language. In D. R. Olson & N. Torrance (Eds.), *The Cambridge handbook of literacy* (pp. 112–133). New York: Cambridge University Press.

Spinelli, C. G. (2008). Addressing the issue of cultural and linguistic diversity and assessment: Informal evaluation measures for English language learners. *Reading and Writing Quarterly, 24*(1), 101–118.

Squires, D. A. (2009). *Curriculum alignment: Research-based strategies for increasing student achievement.* Newbury Park, CA: Corwin Press.

Stahl, K. A. D., & McKenna, M. C. (2012). *Reading assessment in an RTI framework.* New York: Guilford Press.

Stein, M. K., & Nelson, B. S. (2003). Leadership content knowledge. *Educational Evaluation and Policy Analysis, 25*(4), 423–448.

Taylor, J. A., Getty, S. R., Kowalski, S. M., Wilson, C. D., Carlson, J., & Van Scotter, P. (2015). An efficacy trial of research-based curriculum materials with curriculum-based professional development. *American Educational Research Journal.*

Terry, N. P., & Connor, C. M. (2012). Changing nonmainstream American English use and early reading achievement from kindergarten to first grade. *American Journal of Speech–Language Pathology, 21,* 78–86.

Torgesen, J., Houston, D., & Rissman, L. (2007). *Improving literacy instruction in middle and high schools: A guide for principals.* Portsmouth, NH: RMC Research Corporation, Center on Instruction.

Townsend, D. (2015). Who's using the language?: Supporting middle school students with content area academic language. *Journal of Adolescent and Adult Literacy, 58*(5), 376–387.

Townsend, D., & Kiernan, D. (2015). Selecting academic vocabulary words worth learning. *The Reading Teacher, 69*(1), 113–118.

Uccelli, P., Phillips Galloway, E. P., Barr, C. D., Meneses, A., & Dobbs, C. L. (2015). Beyond vocabulary: Exploring cross disciplinary academic language proficiency and its association with reading comprehension. *Reading Research Quarterly, 50*(3), 337–356.

Valencia, S. W., & Buly, M. R. (2004). Behind test scores: What struggling readers really need. *The Reading Teacher, 57*(6), 520–533.

Valencia, S. W., Wixson, K. K., & Pearson, P. D. (2014). Putting text complexity in context. *The Elementary School Journal, 115*(2), 270–289.

van Lier, L., & Walqui, A. (2012). Language and the Common Core State Standards. In K. Hakuta & M. Santos (Eds.), *Understanding language: Commissioned papers on language and literacy issues in the Common Core State Standards and Next Generation Science Standards* (pp. 1–133). Stanford, CA: Stanford University.

Vaughn, S., Klingner, J. K., Swanson, E. A., Boardman, A. G., Roberts, G., Mohammed, S. S., et al. (2011). Efficacy of collaborative strategic reading with middle school students. *American Educational Research Journal, 48*(4), 938–964.

Vaughn, S., Roberts, G., Swanson, E. A., Wanzek, J., Fall, A. M., & Stillman-Spisak, S. J. (2015). Improving middle-school students' knowledge and comprehension in social studies: A replication. *Educational Psychology Review, 27*(1), 31–50.

Villegas-Reimers, E. (2003). *Teacher professional development: An international review of the literature.* Paris: International Institute for Educational Planning.

Vipond, D., & Hunt, R. A. (1984). Point-driven understanding: Pragmatic and cognitive dimensions of literary reading. *Poetics, 13*(3), 261–277.

Washington, J. A., Terry, N. P., & Seidenberg, M. S. (2013). Language variation and literacy learning: The case of African American English. In C. A. Stone, E. R. Silliman, B. J. Ehren, & K. Apel (Eds.), *Handbook of language and literacy: Development and disorders* (2nd ed., pp. 204–221). New York: Guilford Press.

Waters, T., Marzano, R. J., & McNulty, B. (2003). *Balanced leadership: What 30 years of research tells us about the effect of leadership on student achievement.* Aurora, CO: Mid-Continent Research for Education and Learning.

Wolfram, W., & Schilling-Estes, N. (2005). *American English: Dialects and variation.* Malden, MA: Blackwell.

Woods, A., Dooley, K., Luke, A., & Exley, B. (2014). School leadership, literacy and social justice: The place of local school curriculum planning and reform. In I. Bogotch & C. M. Shields (Eds.), *International handbook of educational leadership and social (in) justice* (pp. 509–520). Dordrecht, The Netherlands: Springer.

Yurdakula, B. (2015). Perceptions of elementary school teachers concerning the concept of curriculum. *Educational Sciences: Theory and Practice, 15*(1), 1–15.

Index

Note: *n* following a page number indicates a note.